D1410582

New
Directions in
German
Architecture

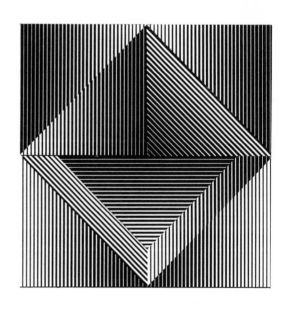

GÜNTHER FEUERSTEIN

NEW DIRECTIONS

IN

GERMAN

ARCHITECTURE

GEORGE BRAZILLER   NEW YORK

Translated by Thomas E. Burton

For information address the publisher:

George Braziller, Inc.

One Park Avenue

New York, N.Y.   10016

Library of Congress Catalog Card No. 68-56282

Designed by Jennie Bush

First Printing

Printed in U.S.A.

CONTENTS

1471209

FOREWORD

To give an account of a country's architecture is to make a choice among an almost infinite number of possibilities. This choice should not be dogmatic but is necessarily subjective; today's critic can no longer rely on universally accepted criteria. Important trends, whatever their true quality, should not be omitted, yet the choice should not be confined to the "best" architects or buildings. Above all, it can never reflect the entire range of general building activity.

It has not been possible to include a full discussion of the state of the German cities since the urban environment is the subject of controversy and criticism so extensive that it could not be contained within the bounds of this book.

The influences at work in German architecture are numerous and sometimes contradictory, so that for the visitor the first impression is of a bright mosaic of contrasting trends, some vital and vigorous, some merely derivative or fashionable. German architecture is held in a taut but shifting balance between the two poles of a powerful field of force: on the one hand is the awareness that architectural motivations are to a large extent sociological and political, on the other the legitimate desire for "expression," diversity and identification, formal organization, and aesthetic quality. In between stand the requirements of technology and the logic of construction. These factors, though divergent, are not necessarily irreconcilable, and the younger generation of German architects may well be on the way toward a new synthesis. Admittedly, this synthesis is constantly being obstructed by the demands of the "powers that be" (industry, politics, wealth) for representation and due recognition; that is, for a prestige architecture which has little to do with the ideals of the new society.

Thus, architecture, too, is destined to play a part in the great intellectual, social, and economic debate whose climax is clearly now at hand.

THE FIRST HALF OF THE CENTURY

THE end of the nineteenth century coincided with the end of a controversial but impressive architectural period—the period of historicism. Since about 1830 European design and fashion had imitated historical styles in an archaeological, patriotic, and bourgeois manner. In Germany, the new ideas derived from engineering and a revolutionary industrial aesthetic, which were introduced around 1900, were only hesitantly accepted. Jugendstil, the German version of Art Nouveau, while vigorously rejecting historicism, restored to prominence the ideas of "art" and craftsmanship, without doing much to integrate architecture with technology.

The first great period of modern architecture began in 1910 with expressionism, which had already been heralded in the innovations of Jugendstil and relied heavily upon the achievements of the Deutscher Werkbund, an association of young manufacturers, architects, artists, and writers, founded in 1907. Theodor Fischer, Paul Bonatz, Hans Poelzig, and Bernhard Hoetger were among the leading representatives of this emotionally inspired architecture.

The transition from historicism and expressionism to the novel concepts of rationalism and functionalism can be illustrated by a few selected examples: the A.E.G. Turbine Factory in Berlin by Peter Behrens (1909), the Water Tower at Posen by Hans Poelzig (1911), and the Centenary Hall in Breslau by Max Berg (1912–1913). Despite this infiltration of rational elements, expressionism survived into the years immediately following the First World War, as seen by Eric Mendelsohn's Einstein Tower in Potsdam (1919–1921). But with the construction of Walter Gropius' Model Factory at the 1914 Werkbund Exhibition in Cologne, the pendulum began to swing strongly in the direction of functionalism and a technical aesthetic.

In 1919, Gropius embodied these ideas in the design of a school that was to win worldwide acclaim—the Staatliche Bauhaus, an institution initially concerned with the synthesis of art, handcrafts, and architecture, but quick to appreciate the relevance of modern technology to this ideal. In 1930, the prominent artists who taught at the Bauhaus were joined by one of Germany's greatest architects, Mies van der Rohe. Mies, too, had gone through an expressionist phase, but by 1922 his designs already displayed a mastery of an architectonic and structural vocabulary that has lost none of its validity even today. In the space of two years, Mies produced two buildings that were to become classics of international architecture: in 1927, the site plan and four-story apartment house at the Weissenhof community near Stuttgart and in 1929, the German Pavilion for the International Exhibition in Barcelona. The originality of the Weissenhofsiedlung, designed in collaboration with sixteen of Europe's leading architects, lay in the coordination of its vigorously articulated cubes, while the Barcelona Pavilion offered a new concept of architectural space. Here space was no longer shaped or closed; panels and slabs created undefinable open areas. The Tugendhat house (1930) in Brno, Czechoslovakia, modified this new conception of space; it also marked the end of the architect's European career. In 1937 he immigrated to the United States, there to continue his creative activities.

Gropius and Mies played a decisive part in the development of the International Style in the twenties, particularly its "white cube" phase. The focal point of this new architecture was Berlin, where Gropius and Mies shared their influence with Hans Scharoun —one of the few whose reputation was to survive the Second World War, Hugo Häring, an exponent of organic, nonrectangular building, and Eric Mendelsohn, whose early free-form work and later geometric buildings linked expressionism and the International Style.

This lively and spirited development, which took place despite the economic and political turbulence of the times, came to an abrupt end when Hitler seized power in 1933. Numerous well-known architects were forced to emigrate for "racial reasons" or left the country of their own accord. Others vainly attempted to come to an understanding with the new rulers. Fascism could tolerate only two kinds of state architecture: a monumental, politically totalitarian classicism and a sentimentally heroic "blood and soil" style of a nationalistic stamp. Among the accomplishments of the more tractable who submitted to the guidance of the state there is scarcely anything of distinction, except perhaps Werner March's Olympic Stadium or the traditionalist buildings of Heinrich Tessenow.

To be sure, the groundwork for Hitlerian architecture had been laid earlier by the adherents of monumental expressionism and the sentimental Heimatstil (a national-romantic and traditionalist variation of Art Nouveau, often in a cheerfully rustic vein). These rudiments were played up and sent gloriously into battle against "Jewish-Bolshevist-International" architecture. Thus was instilled the sterile creed of an anachronistic state architecture. Shaking off this legacy was to prove one of the hardest tasks for the postwar generation of German architects.

POWER AND SIMPLICITY—
EXPRESSIVE TRENDS

After the Second World War

A T THE end of the Second World War Germany lay in ruins. The sites of once flourishing historic cities were now marked by piles of rubble. This material destruction, however, had long been preceded by the destruction of intellectual and artistic heritage. In 1933 the lively development of contemporary German architecture, the equal of anything on the international scene, was cut short, like all German art, by the dictates of fascism.

After the Second World War the material resources were replenished more rapidly than the stock of ideas. Thus, the period from 1945 to about 1955 was characterized by a cautious searching and groping, a state of mind that prevailed not only in Germany but throughout Europe. If one is to do justice to the buildings of the period, one must not lose sight of the difficulties of that decade. For political reasons there could be no continuation of fascist classicism or the architectural ideology of "blood and soil." Thus architects avoided the formal language of a politically manipulated architecture, but the totalitarian spirit was less easily suppressed and lived on, somewhat diluted, in numerous representative structures.

There seemed to be an inability or a disinclination to restore the situation of the thirties, because of the deeply rooted suspicion of that period, whose quality was only gradually discovered later. Many of its masters had emigrated, others were dead. In many instances Germany's neighbors had also been caught up in the wake of fascist architecture, even those who had remained more or less politically independent.

Architects accepted ideas from Scandinavia and Switzerland most readily. The tendency in those countries was to avoid extreme formulas in favor of a pleasant, casual, and humane architecture, which contrasted sharply with the monumental pseudo-classicism of the totalitarian systems.

Among the vague and shifting developments of the first postwar decade it is possible to discern a few characteristic trends. Though scarcely significant at the evolutionary level, they can fairly claim to represent a specifically German architecture.

In the years immediately following the war, American influence was particularly strong. Intellectual and personal contact between America and Germany was fostered by two prominent personalities of the period between the wars: Walter Gropius and Mies van der Rohe. Both were intimately connected with the activity of the Bauhaus in Weimar and Dessau, both emigrated and found a rich new field for their talents in the United States. True, their personal and direct intervention in behalf of German architecture came only very late and on a limited scale: in 1957 Gropius built an apartment house for the Berlin Interbau (International Building Exhibition), and in 1960 he supplied the basic plan for the Britz-Buckow-Rudow residential development, also in Berlin, which in fact became severely criticized for its derivative, incoherent form (see "City Planning," pp. 67–78). In 1963 Mies, still remembered for his magnificent achievement of the twenties, the Weissenhof community, was commissioned to design the Museum Moderner Kunst in Berlin. Mature, classical, the last word of a great master, this building marks the end of a development.

Nevertheless, Mies's work and American structuralism began indirectly to influence Germany soon after the war (cf. *Figs. 1–2*). Here, it was thought, was a versatile tool for solving all kinds of problems. If Mies's quality was rarely approached, it was because in Germany he had many imitators, but no students. Only too often his thoroughly aesthetic technicism was perverted by tasteless excess and superficial decoration.

Commercial Structuralism

The significant transition from structure to skin, from load-bearing frame to curtain wall, long a feature of the modern American office building, has its imitators in Germany. Maximum transparency and an almost feminine fragility push toward the limits of immateriality, while a gradually solidifying prosperity seeks self-expression in visible symbols of the German "economic miracle." As in America, so in Germany the glass box and the curtain wall are standard elements in office building design.

The most important commercial structure of the early period of development is undoubtedly the Thyssen Building (Phönix-Rheinrohr Building, *Fig. 1*) in Düsseldorf, designed by Helmut Hentrich and Hubert Petschnigg and dating from 1957 to 1960. Its cleavage into three staggered, connecting slabs is a notable attempt to break away from the anonymous box of the conventional skyscraper.

While the Thyssen Building owes its originality to the resolution of the masses, the Mannesmann Building (*Fig. 2*), also in Düsseldorf and designed by Paul Schneider-Esleben in 1952, achieves a similar effect by the subtle proportions of the details and the building as a whole, and by the harmonious choice of materials, both inside and out. The outside curtain wall is of aluminum with blue-white steel panels, and the inside includes aluminum, dark leather, and wood.

These office buildings set an architectural standard which has scarcely been equaled. Even the interesting play of levels found in the Europa Center in Berlin (1963–1965), a later Hentrich-Petschnigg design, cannot altogether compensate for its conventional skyscraper conception, and the structure reflects a stagnation of development

1. *Helmut Hentrich and Hubert Petschnigg: Thyssen Building (Phönix-Rheinrohr Building), Düsseldorf, 1957–60.*

2. *Paul Schneider-Esleben: Mannesmann Building, Düsseldorf, 1952.*

3. *Walter Henn and Dieter Ströbel with Osram Munich office: Osram Building, Munich, 1963–65.*

which must also share the blame for the failure of integration of single building and city in urban design.

The ultimate refinement of the glass curtain wall is exemplified in a Munich office building designed by Walter Henn (with Dieter Ströbel; *Fig. 3*). Its graphic two-dimensionality is so obviously the end state of an evolutionary process that it immediately enlists one's sympathy for a new aesthetic or material differentiation.

In the IBM Building in Berlin (*Fig. 4*), Rolf Gutbrod offers an interesting example of this genre. The bland skin is replaced by a tiered or banded effect with strong horizontal emphasis, which also lends relief to the facades. The elegant wall panels and the superior finish bear comparison with the polish achieved by the Italians.

Werner Düttmann (with Karl-Heinz Fischer) has staggered the Urania Office Building in Berlin (*Fig. 5*) both in plan and in elevation, thus making the most of the shape of the lot. The powerful articulation of the building as a whole is sustained by the rhythmic and delicate elements of the facade; here the trend toward an architecture of plastic relief is obvious.

A notable though disputed attempt to revitalize the administrative building has been made by the architects A. G. Atmer, J. Marlow, H. T. Holthey, H. Freese, and E. Jux. Their Police Headquarters in Hamburg (*Fig. 6*) has a repetitive facade deliberately interrupted by "interfering elements" which are at once atypical and functionally symbolic. The courtroom has been emphasized, and symbolic elements are employed to underscore its significance.

If lively surface relief is one way of progressing beyond the classical glass box, breaking up the masses is another. In the Siemens Building in Düsseldorf (Siemenswerke Building Department; chief architect, Petersen), the perfect flatness of the metal curtain wall is compensated for by a brisk jog in the street front.

Thus, the desire to modify the commercial rationalism of the fifties, while continuing to satisfy necessary functional requirements of utility, communication and traffic patterns, working conditions, and economy, is evident.

Symbols of Power

There are, however, other aspects to consider concerning large public buildings. In a country gradually regaining its strength after a disastrous war, the new holders of power and influence crave suitable representation and expression. Although the traditional media of representation are rejected, on another plane attributes that justify references to a classicistic-representational approach are admitted.

Thus, in Hans Maurer's office building on the Königinstrasse in Munich (*Fig. 7*), the effort to impose a tight order is apparent even in the plan, which is governed by the classical ratio of three to five bays. The axiality of the entrance is reinforced by the atypical end bays of the facade, which reach beyond repetitive harmony toward a measurable symmetry. The proximity of a classical building of the

4. *Rolf Gutbrod and Bernhard Binder with Helmut Bätzner, Hans Holch, and Horst Schaderer: IBM Building, West Berlin, 1962.*

5. *Werner Düttmann with Karl-Heinz Fischer: Urania Office Building, West Berlin, 1964–67.*

early nineteenth century would make these elements appear not to be mere chance.

It is natural that government buildings should be particularly sensitive to pressures for a representative architecture. Like so many reconstructions, the Provincial Parliament Building in Hanover (*Fig. 8*), designed by Dieter Oesterlen, has had to reconcile itself to an existing historical situation. Insistence on an image of solemn dignity could bring architecture dangerously close to a monumental state art of the totalitarian variety.

The desire to project a fitting image is shared by cultural as well as political and economic groups. Because of the intimate relationship between society and drama, the new theaters serve as social indicators of taste and status. Fritz Bornemann's German Opera in Berlin and the Gelsenkirchen City Theater (*Fig. 9*; Werner Ruhnau, Ortwin Rave, and Max von Hausen) reflect the German "affluent society's" demand for recognition, as expressed through the medium of new temples of the muses. It is significant that none of the large theaters provides an essentially new type of stage. Of course, the fine arts—painting and sculpture—are allowed to occupy their intellectual niche, but all too often they serve merely as window dressing, evidence of the supposed cultural awareness of the patrons.

This is the snare of cultural posturing that Klaus Gessler seeks to avoid in his new theater in Bonn (*Fig. 10*), a building which derives its character from the way in which the asymmetrical axes are

6. *A. G. Atmer, J. Marlow, H. T. Holthey, H. Freese, and E. Jux: Police Headquarters, Hamburg, 1958–66.*

7. *Hans Maurer: Offices for Münchner Rückversicherung, Königinstrasse, Munich, 1963–65.*
8. *Dieter Oesterlen: Lower Saxony Provincial Parliament Building, Hanover, 1957–62.*

9. *Werner Ruhnau, Ortwin Rave, and Max v. Hausen: City theater, Gelsenkirchen, 1958–59.*

10. *Klaus Gessler and W. Beck with P. Frohne, R. Wagner, and H. Griese: City theater, Bonn, 1962–65.*

11. *Hardt-Waltherr Hämer and W. B. Hämer-Buro with Meyer-Rogge, Weber: CityTheater, Ingolstadt, 1962–66.*

resolved and in which oblique shapes are used for an irregular, lively appearance.

Hardt-Waltherr Hämer has dealt beautifully with the dilemma of prestige versus social obligation in his Ingolstadt City Theater (*Fig. 11*). This building, with its excellent plastic and spatial articulation, allows plenty of room for the public without entertaining any particular preconceptions about the strata of society from which it will be drawn. The use of simple concrete surfaces and the lively handling of space create an exciting ambiance that can well dispense with the attributes of prosperity.

Luxury, Simplicity, Ethos

What, then, is the course to steer between the blossoming prosperity of a society of plenty, and concern for the essentials of architecture and of life, which for the present generation means, first, the full development of the free and total human personality encouraged by the environment, that is by architecture; second, proper respect for sociological and political values, which in building find expression, above all, in urban design; and, third, the new concepts of volume, space and plasticity? The answer does not lie in villas and summer homes nor in American-style office buildings.

In building, the situation in the early postwar period, before the economic recovery of the fifties really began, was one of acute distress. In spite of this, there were few attempts to achieve substantial economies in architectural means, and the virtues of austerity became even less appealing with the arrival of the boom. Nevertheless, for their youth hostel in Odersbach (*Fig. 12*), Tassilo Sittmann and Walter Schwagenscheidt decided upon a rough but thoroughly appealing frugality. There is almost an air of improvisation, of the primitive and makeshift; at any rate, it is conceivable that this building could tolerate a variety of spontaneous rearrangements, additions, and extensions without the "architecture" being destroyed. A romantic trait, perhaps—indeed the architects freely admit it—but also a clear expression of the permanent tension that exists in German architecture between the dual elements of romanticism and rationalism.

Among other early examples of a disciplined austerity with intense spatial differentiation (for instance, strong articulation or cleavaçe into cubic parts) are the buildings of Hans C. Müller and Georg Heinrichs. The parish hall of the Friedenskirche (*Fig. 13*) and the Eichkamp student housing in Berlin are excellent illustrations of this approach. Otherwise, among the self-conscious pretensions of the Establishment and the helpless banality of countless run-of-the-mill buildings, deliberate intellectual choices in favor of economy of means are rare indeed. Perhaps they are reflected in the work of Ernst von Rudloff—for example, his church of St. Bonifatius in Gelsenkirchen-Buer (*Fig. 14*)—or in that of Werner Düttmann (St. Agnes in Berlin, *Fig 15*; Berlin Technical University Dining Hall).

Any mention of the thoughtful, morally responsible basis of

12. *Walter Schwagenscheidt and Tassilo Sittmann with E. Hofmann: Youth hostel, Odersbach, 1960.*

13. *Hans C. Müller and Georg Heinrichs: Friedenskirche Parish Hall, West Berlin, 1961.*

14. *Ernst von Rudloff: St. Bonifatius, Gelsenkirchen-Buer, 1966–67.*
15. *Werner Düttmann: St. Agnes Catholic Church and Community Center, West Berlin, 1965–66.*

German architecture must include a reference to Egon Eiermann, the most important personality among postwar German architects, although he has recently retired somewhat into the background. Despite his highly refined visual statements, Eiermann always remains true to a structural logic, thus creating a solid basis for a wide variety of projects. His solutions are never dogmatic but, rather, coherent stages in a lively development.

The handkerchief factory in Blumberg, 1951, is an example of a subtly handled industrial plant. In the Neckermann Mail-Order House in Frankfurt (*Fig. 16*), the powerful dialectic between cubic motifs and the linear, two-dimensional treatment of the facade raises this building far above the utilitarian level.

The German pavilion at the 1958 Brussels Exposition (designed with Sep Ruf) should be mentioned in connection with Eiermann's development toward extreme transparency combined with three-dimensionality. Webs of delicate structural members are spun around loose constellations of wholly transparent cubes of unsurpassed aesthetic quality in structural dimension, proportion, and finish.

St. Matthew in Pforzheim was designed in 1953 by Eiermann, whose use here of square, precast concrete elements may have been inspired by Auguste Perret's church in Le Raincy, France (1922). Although the exterior is quite unostentatious, the interior is of convincing clarity and austerity. The simplicity of this place of

16. *Egon Eiermann: Neckermann Mail-Order House, Frankfurt, 1958–60.*

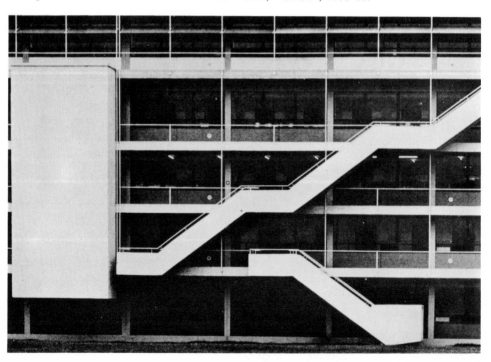

worship, one of the most remarkable churches in Germany, stands in contrast with the imposing structure of Eiermann's Memorial Church in Berlin (*Fig. 17*) of 1959–1963. Here, too, precast concrete elements are employed, but they are double-walled, glazed with dark blue glass and illuminated from the inside to produce a spectacular effect—both by day and by night—which could be interpreted as a modern equivalent of the "diaphanous" walls of the Gothic cathedrals. The church stands next to the ruined tower of the old Kaiser Wilhelm Memorial Church, destroyed in the Second World War, but a second, new tower has been built close by, expressly to document the fact that even the present age is capable of raising symbols.

Church Architecture

Egon Eiermann's two churches in Pforzheim and Berlin have already served to illustrate some of the most important elements of religious architecture: accommodation of congregation, space, light, structural concept, and building technique. To these must be added, at least as far as the Catholic faith is concerned, problems connected with the new liturgy.

Of the architects of the prewar generation, only one, Rudolf Schwarz, has succeeded in maintaining a strict continuity in his church design from the thirties to the present. The Corpus Christi Church (Fronleichnamskirche) in Aachen (1928), one of the first

17. *Egon Eiermann with R. Wiest: Memorial Church, West Berlin, 1959–63.*

"non-mystic" churches, was a milestone in his development, to be followed after the war by buildings such as St. Anne in Düren (1951) and St. Michael in Frankfurt (1953; *Fig. 18*), that document his masterly handling of space. The large, noble room of St. Michael was economically built and is excellently lit by natural daylight.

Though they survived the war, the other two pioneers of early modern church architecture, Otto Bartning and Dominikus Böhm, failed to produce any trend-setting designs in their later years.

Dominikus Böhm's son, Gottfried Böhm, has inherited much of his father's spirit. For him, too, a church is vastly more than a functional meeting place; it must have spatial qualities of a purely expressive kind. The Catholic Pilgrims Church in Neviges (1966–1968; *Fig. 19*) is typical of his approach. Space has been resolved into forms that have no visible geometric order or system of measurement, and the complex faceting of walls and ceiling mark the transition to a sculptural architecture. Though it may be inappropriate to speak of neo-expressionism, since the cultural and intellectual milieu differs now from that of fifty years ago, the motifs that determine space and form are undoubtedly suprarational.

18. *Rudolf Schwarz: St. Michael, Frankfurt am Main, 1953.*

It is natural that expressive architecture should flourish specifically in church building, with its predominant spiritual demands.
In Dieter Baumewerd's Church of the Holy Spirit in Emmerich am
Niederrhein (*Figs. 20–21*), the structural elements—giant reinforced
concrete mushrooms—create a bizarre silhouette. Inside the church,
their varying heights are the source of a richly differentiated play
of light. Fred Thieler's large murals contribute importantly to the
spatial effect.

The relations between tower and nave, solid concrete walls
and window slits, and interior light and darkness are the basic
themes of Helmut Striffler's churches. The Church on the Blumenau,
Mannheim (*Fig. 22*) is dominated by the vigorous pitch of the roof,

19 *Gottfried Böhm: Pilgrims Church, Neviges, 1966–68.*

20. *Dieter Baumewerd: Church of the Holy Spirit, Emmerich am Niederrhein, 1965–66, interior.*
21. *Church of the Holy Spirit, exterior.*

22. *Helmut Striffler: Church on the Blumenau, Mannheim, 1961.*
23. *Helmut Striffler: Memorial Chapel, Dachau, 1967.*

while the Protestant Memorial Chapel at the former Dachau concentration camp (*Fig. 23*) is distinguished by a rich variety in the sequence of its rooms and spaces.

Among the most important works in the volumetric expressive idiom are those of Rainer Disse. St. Elizabeth in Freiburg (*Fig. 24*) manages to avoid being merely a spectacular feat of acrobatics in concrete and extracts a high degree of quality from structure, function, and the disposition of the masses.

Mature handling of the concrete volumes, especially around the entrance, is a feature of the church of St. Otto in Speyer (*Fig. 25*), designed by a cooperative composed of the architects Wolfgang Hirsch, Rudolf Hoinkis, Martin Lanz, Paul Schütz, and Dieter Stahl (with H. Linde).

Klaus Franz has based his design of a church for the Catholic Maria Regina Parish Center in Fellbach near Stuttgart (*Fig. 26*) on the simple geometrical shape of the truncated cone, thus attempting to line the solemnity of the lighting with the idea of the parish.

The university chapels in Bochum, designed by Fritz Eller, Erich Moser, and Robert Walter, could well be a notable contribution to church architecture. Despite the strictly modular plan, the controlled progression of heights creates a strong formal dominant that simultaneously expresses the relationship between the great Christian faiths, the Protestant and Catholic. Berlin's Regina Martyrum, a church designed by Johannes Schädel, is a grand and ambitious

24. *Rainer Disse: St. Elizabeth, Freiburg, 1964–66.*

25. *Wolfgang Hirsch, Rudolf Hoinkis, Martin Lanz, Paul Schütz, and Dieter Stahl with H. Linde: St. Otto, Speyer, 1964.*

26. *Klaus Franz: Maria Regina Parish Center, Fellbach, Stuttgart, 1965–67.*

structure, but many of its details have not been thought out as carefully as a project on this scale requires.

Carlfried Mutschler's work illustrates his progression from the use of glass and simple ground plans to the closed, chunky solidity of concrete cubes; the former is represented by the Pfingstberg Church in Mannheim, the latter by St. Luke, which forms part of the Protestant Parish Center at Mannheim-Neckarau (*Fig. 27*).

In the church designed by H. Kuhn and Friedhelm Grundmann (*Fig. 28*), Hamburg, the pathos of monumental expressionism in concrete has receded somewhat. Le Corbusier's sculptural prototype has been modified to a more structural, stereometric concept, and the relationship between the concrete structure and the white cubes is expressed in a striking play of light and shade, which is effectively continued in the interior.

Brutalism and Differentiation of Form

The expressionist element in German church architecture is not an isolated phenomenon but has a parallel in the international trend sympathetic to or derived from the Brutalism of the postwar period. Yet the German version of this trend stems in part from developments peculiar to Germany. As already mentioned, dissatisfaction with the smooth glass box led first to plastic accentuation of the facade. Emphasis on individual building elements, not always structurally justified, was used to create relief, and from this a more fluid concept of the facade was gradually derived. Hans Joachim Lenz (with Eugen Müller) demonstrate this aproach in the Ketteler College in Mainz (*Fig. 29*).

The end result of the trend is a rich differentiation of form, generally expressed in Brutalist concrete cubes. The criteria are not merely the use of exposed concrete, which gradually becomes a cliché, but the intellectual drive toward more powerful "expression" and the disclosure of structural honesty.

This concern for a recognizable statement leads to the realm of the literary and symbolic, to the very borderline of romanticism and architectural showmanship, indeed to mannerism. Peripheral motifs are overemphasized and monumentalized.

A consequence of this, or at least an associated symptom, is a heavy concentration of sculpturally articulated masses. This style, which has certain parallels in some Swiss buildings and in American East Coast architecture, might be described as "compact-differentiated." It is a style that has appealed to a large number of progressive architects in the sixties.

A very personal version of concrete-cube Brutalism is being developed by Joachim Schürmann. He avoids the temptations to perfectionism associated with this trend, which has turned from the frugal, coarse style of the fifties to a "pretty" surface finish. He knows how to work on a grand scale without being pompous. The

27. *Carlfried Mutschler: St. Luke, part of Protestant Parish Center, Mannheim-Neckarau, 1965–66.*

28. *Friedhelm Grundmann and H. Kuhn: St. Simeon, Hamburg, 1966.*

29. *Hans Joachim Lenz with Eugen Müller: Ketteler College, Mainz, 1964.*
30. *Joachim Schürmann: Monastery of St. Sebastian, Cologne/Neuss, 1967.*

controlled handling of space and volume in the monastery of St. Sebastian near Cologne (*Fig. 30*) is reminiscent of anonymous Mediterranean architecture, an impression further strengthened by the whitewashed surfaces. His high school in Beuel is likewise remarkable for the excellent relationship between cube and open space.

Compact-differentiated architecture, with its insistence on the qualities of materials, is also of interest to Germans from another viewpoint. Concern for the preservation and logical restoration of historic buildings and neighborhoods is a special preoccupation, and it is easier to make additions to these in an architectural language which—in an entirely positive sense—is determined by an intense romantic-emotional component. In this form, "modern" architecture is more palatable to the population at large.

Gottfried Böhm's town hall at Bensberg (*Fig. 31*) affords an excellent example. The new concrete structure is attached to the old castle, but the joint is seamless. The transition is equally smooth in Dieter Oesterlen's Historical Museum in Hanover (*Fig. 32*), in which one of the decisive factors is again the structure and scale of existing ancient timbered buildings.

A "bizarre concrete structure" are the words used by architect Günter Bock himself to describe his community center at Sindlingen near Frankfurt am Main (*Fig. 33*). Indeed, the telescoping of the staggered concrete forms creates a lively silhouette, and the virtuoso handling of the facade recalls the De Stijl movement in Holland. The claims made by the building are no doubt sociologically justified, but they derive as well from the desire for a visible symbol with which the residents of the area can identify. This was once the exclusive function of the town hall, but today community buildings are also regarded as a means of expressing the power and importance of the citizenry.

Similar pretensions sometimes characterize commissions executed for church organizations. The library towers of Paul Schneider-Esleben's building for the editorial offices of a Catholic press (*Fig. 34*) ascend with almost sacred solemnity. The accentuated, richly articulated concrete forms and the use of the 60° angle create an expressive structure whose outward "significance" considerably overreaches its actual content.

The transition to architectonic and sculptural principles is exemplified in a home for the aged by Reinhard Gieselmann (*Fig. 35*). A consistent solution of a Brutalist stamp is to be found in a minor building by a younger architect: the filter house of the Limburg Baths (*Fig. 36*) by Johannes Peter Hölzinger.

On the other hand, there have been numerous modifications and dilutions of Brutalism in favor of a more subtle development of detail, more refined surface treatment, and more careful planning.

The problem of striking a balance between an ethos of simplicity and a significant differentiation of volume is one that preoccupies Oswald Mathias Ungers, who has recently had an important

31. *Gottfried Böhm: Town Hall, Bensberg, 1967.*
32. *Dieter Oesterlen: Historical Museum, Hanover, 1962–66.*

33. *Günter Bock: Community Center, Sindlingen, 1961.*
34. *Paul Schneider-Esleben: Stimmen der Zeit editorial offices, Munich, 1966.*

35. *Reinhard Gieselmann: Home for the aged (under direction of the German Red Cross), Karlsruhe, 1964–66.*

36. *Johannes Peter Hölzinger: Filter house, Baths, Limburg, 1961.*

influence on the Berlin architectural scene. His own home is a masterly example. It is more severe and taut than similar buildings in the eastern United States; in fact, it is more closely related to Dutch architecture, an impression strengthened by the disciplined use of brick. However, the techniques of lively plastic articulation, firmly integrated with the functional, are also masterfully employed in larger projects such as the housing in Cologne (*Figs. 37–38*).

Dissatisfaction with the Right Angle

The new device of breaking up masses into cubes, combined with a more vigorous treatment of the building, did not long suffice. Architects began to insist on a broader vocabulary of forms transcending rectangularity. In Klaus Gessler's City Theater in Bonn (*Fig. 10*), in H. W. Hämer's Ingolstadt City Theater (*Fig. 11*), and in Dieter Baumewerd's churches (*Figs. 20 –21*), the oblique angle is already in evidence. In his editorial offices in Munich (*Fig. 34*), Paul Schneider-Esleben works with triangles and hexagons. Similarly, the triangle is the basic geometrical motif of the plan of Brunswick City Hall (Peter Voigtländer). In Gottfried Böhm's buildings (*Figs. 19, 31*), the complex development of space and plan depends on the use of a variety of diagonals and broken planes.

However, it is in buildings with spiritual claims that go beyond strict functionalism that particularly vigorous attempts are being made to escape the alleged rationality of the right angle. A typical example of this is Ulrich S. von Altenstadt's cultural center for Leverkusen (*Fig. 41*). The sprightly silhouette of the roof and the use of the 120° angle create a lively architectural landscape.

If the use of jogs and facets is one means of breaking away from the right angle, the rounded undulating form is another, though one less frequently employed. Bernhard Pfau's theater in Düsseldorf (*Figs. 39–40*) successfully reconciles plan requirements and formal conception. Other examples can be taken from church architecture —for instance, Carlfried Mutschler's hospital chapel in Mannheim (*Fig. 42*) or Joachim Schürmann's star-shaped church in Neuss (*Fig. 43*).

The preoccupation with a dynamic architecture is apparent in a relatively early structure, the Stuttgart Concert Hall or Liederhalle built in 1955–1956 from the designs of Adolf Abel and Rolf Gutbrod. In spite of the undeniable interest of the plan and the superabundance of different architectural motifs, the labored attempts to integrate with the architecture the work of various artists and craftsmen are scarcely intelligible today, though quite representative of the situation in the fifties.

The dominance of the oblique angle and so-called free form go hand in hand with a fascination for the geometry of the circle. Ralf Schüler and Ursulina Witte exploit this geometry in a design for the Berlin Transportation Museum (*Fig. 44*).

The adventurous movement away from the restraints of a rec-

37. *Oswald Mathias Ungers: Housing development, Cologne-Seeberg, 1965–66.*
38. *Oswald Mathias Ungers: Housing development, Cologne-Nippes, 1957.*

39. *Bernhard Pfau: Theater, Düsseldorf, 1967–69, model.*
40. *Theater, plan.*

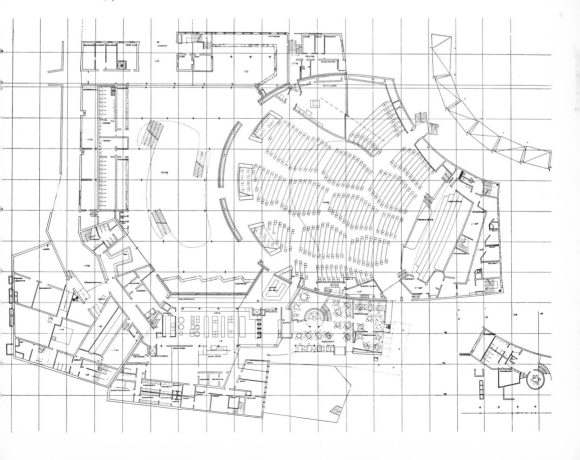

41. *Ulrich S. von Altenstadt: Cultural center, Leverkusen, 1968.*
42. *Carlfried Mutschler: City hospitals' chapel, Mannheim, 1966.*

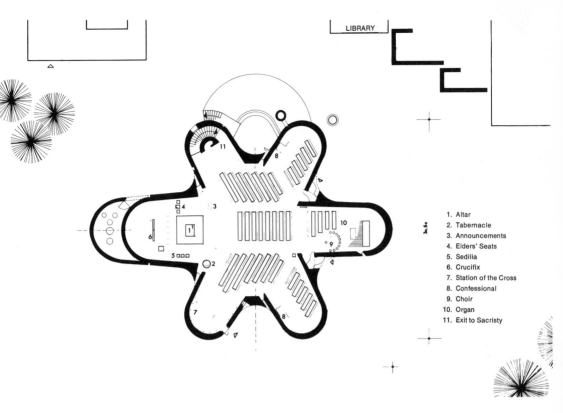

LIBRARY

1. Altar
2. Tabernacle
3. Announcements
4. Elders' Seats
5. Sedilia
6. Crucifix
7. Station of the Cross
8. Confessional
9. Choir
10. Organ
11. Exit to Sacristy

43. *Joachim Schürmann: St. Pius X, Neuss, 1966, plan.*

44. *Ralf Schüler and Ursulina Witte: Transportation Museum, West Berlin, 1968, proposal (model).*

45. *Hans Scharoun (with Wilhelm Frank): "Romeo and Juliet" apartment blocks, Stuttgart, 1954–59, elevation.*

46. *"Romeo and Juliet" apartment blocks, plan.*

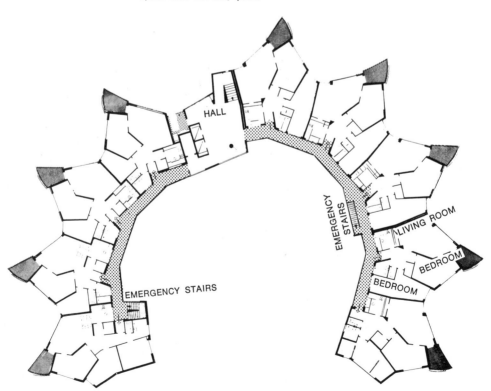

tangular and rational architecture finds full expression in the life work of a great master, Hans Scharoun. Scharoun, one of the greatest figures in the last half-century of German architecture, is also one of the very few to have maintained a continuity of development from the twenties to the present day. Even in his early period, he demonstrated an ability to use the broad gestures of dynamic curves to achieve organic form. By any standards Scharoun penetrates deeply into the essential problems of design and the social implications of architecture and strives for new qualities in all his buildings, public and private. In 1955 he designed the Charlottenburg-Nord development, a lively variation on the row-house theme, and more recently in Stuttgart (with Wilhelm Frank) the "Romeo and Juliet" apartment blocks (*Figs. 45–46*).

Hans Scharoun's best-known building, an international classic, is the Berlin Philharmonic Concert Hall (*Figs. 47–49*). Too much emphasis has been laid on its formal qualities—and shortcomings—while, as we shall see, the immanent principle has been overlooked, though it actually accounts for the importance of this structure. Specifically, Scharoun's achievement can be understood only in terms of the interior spaces. In the auditorium itself a critical contemporary problem, that of the relationship between the collective and the individual in modern society, has been solved. The audience is separated into individual groups which are then "planted out" in a variety of formations and at different levels, like vines in a terraced vineyard. The unity of the ensemble is convincingly restored by the dynamism of the concert hall itself. The same policy of partition and distribution over different levels characterizes the public areas as well. Thus, the building becomes a model for a socially relevant architecture, and the multiple bending, refracting, and faceting of space, the serene handling of oblique angles, and the overlappings and spatial surprises derive their motivation from a comprehensive spatial vision that invincibly absorbs all questions of detail.

In his library, now under construction in Berlin, Scharoun employs very similar means and achieves an animated organic design without having to impose a particular formalism.

In his designs for school buildings (*Figs. 50–51*), Scharoun devised exemplary solutions which were received with great respect but which found few imitators because of their highly personal interpretation. Scharoun envisaged the classroom unit and the whole school as a highly organized "landscape" that not only left room for but positively encouraged a full measure of human activities. Space defined by right angles seemed to him to cramp this creative potential and consequently his spatial principles are expressed, both inside and out, in an abundance of irregularly bent, broken, and angled shapes. The classrooms are not intended simply as teaching areas; thanks to their stimulating atmosphere they are more like temporary homes for the young.

Standards other than those of a classically biased aesthetic are

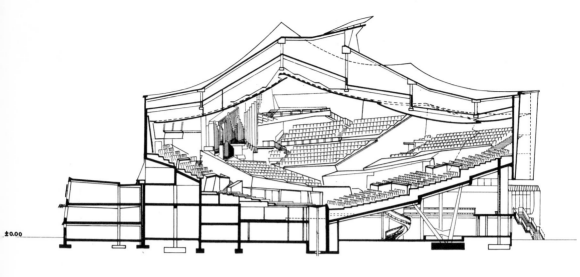

47. *Hans Scharoun: Philharmonic Hall, West Berlin, 1963, section.*

48. *Philharmonic Hall, auditorium plan.*

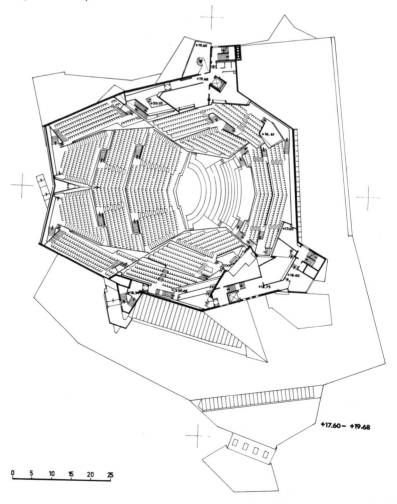

0 5 10 15 20 25

appropriate to the formal domain, and Scharoun knows how to rise above technical perfection with a grand gesture; for him, conventional "good taste" is irrelevant. The external appearance of the buildings—particularly after many years of use—should not be allowed to obscure their quality.

The Geschwister-Scholl School at Lünen in Westphalia is typical of Scharoun's rich spatial vocabulary (*Fig. 50*). His ideas are expressed at an even greater level of complexity in the school at Marl (*Fig. 51*). The classrooms are differentiated according to grade into three groups: lower, middle, and upper. The special areas such as science rooms, home economics rooms, and workshops form compact organic units attached to the classroom groups.

Scharoun himself has no students in the true sense. His architecture does not bear the marks of a reproducible prototype; on the contrary, it is essentially inimitable and in this respect resembles the work of Le Corbusier.

Others also share Scharoun's abhorrence of the right angle and seek a freer and occasionally adventurous language of forms. By spurning the right angle, Sergius Ruegenberg, a contemporary of Scharoun's, has succeeded in acquiring a characteristic spatial vitality. His school in Berlin-Reinickendorf (*Fig. 52*) is an organic concept further enlivened by the overhead lighting of the classrooms. Their research into the nature of the ideal classroom has led architects Johannes Billing, Jens Peters, and Nikolaus Ruff to propose similar nonrectangular groupings for their school in Wildberg (*Fig. 53*).

49. *Philharmonic Hall, interior.*

50. *Hans Scharoun: Geschwister-Scholl School, Westphalia, 1962.*
51. *Hans Scharoun: School, Marl, 1968, plan.*

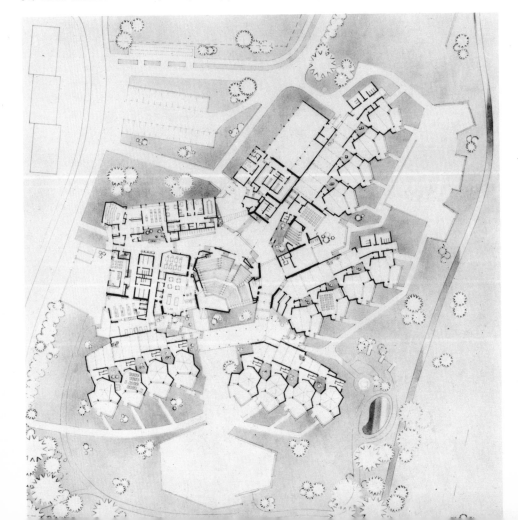

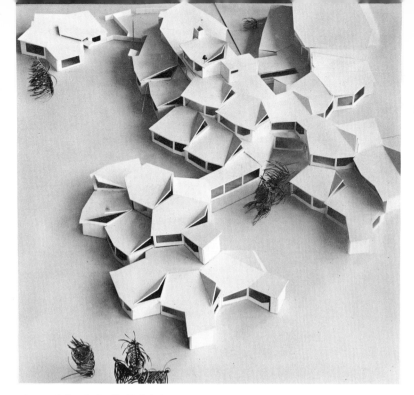

52. *Sergius Ruegenberg: School, Berlin-Reinickendorf, West Berlin, 1967–69.*
53. *Johannes Billing, Jens Peters, and Nikolaus Ruff: School, Wildberg Kreis Calw, 1966–69.*

54. *Wolfgang Hirsch, Rudolf Hoinkis, Martin Lanz, Paul Schütz, and Dieter Stahl: Elementary school, Edenkoben, 1967.*

55. *G. and M. Hänska: Provincial Training School for Medical Technicians, Berlin-Steglitz, West Berlin, 1967.*

Schools and Universities

Like churches, school and college buildings are sensitive indicators of the latest architectural trends. The advance beyond the early postwar "corridor school" in which the classrooms were lined up along narrow corridors, was not only a formal but also a pedagogical and sociological achievement, for which some of the credit, as already pointed out, must go to Hans Scharoun.

The concept of the school as a community is expressed in centralizing and grouping tendencies in which lobbies, halls, and interior courts play an important part. These ideas began to emerge more vigorously toward the end of the fifties.

In the public school at Edenkoben (*Fig. 54*; Wolfgang Hirsch, Rudolf Hoinkis, Martin Lanz, Paul Schütz, and Dieter Stahl, architects), the excellent spatial composition is effectively supported by the terracing of the site, and this three-dimensional conception is extended to individual sculptural elements in the open areas, with the result that spatial continuity is maintained on every scale.

In the Gropiusstadt area of Berlin, a twenty-class primary school has been built by G. and M. Hänska, who have succeeded in showing that the multistory school building also has a considerable potential that can be realized by a free though close-knit grouping of the masses. The same knack for the organization of three-dimensional forms is also displayed in their Provincial Training School for Medical Technicians in Berlin-Steglitz (*Fig. 55*).

In Bedburg, Christoph and Brigitte Parade have built a secondary school which forms an imaginative cluster about a central hall and is further distinguished by the use of powerful concrete elements contrasted with brick. The dominant feature of their high school in Hückelhoven is the array of massive concrete cubes accentuated by diagonal forms. These motifs appear again in a secondary school at Menden (*Fig. 56*), an interesting, extremely compact, and almost fortress-like structure.

The sculptural Brutalism of Hans Joachim Pysall and Eike Rollenhagen is exemplified in a school building at Wolfsburg (*Fig. 57*), which echoes developments in Switzerland—for example, the work of Walter Förderer.

The idea of the school complex is now being carried to a further stage—the school is no longer regarded as an individual building. The emphasis, rather, is on groupings, clusters, and centers which have social as well as educational significance. For example, Harald Deilmann conceived the J. F. Kennedy Educational Center (*Fig. 58*) as an organic grouping around a series of open spaces, thus accomplishing the transition, so important to the modern architect, from the individual "house" to an integral organic community (see "From House to City" in the next chapter).

This development can be followed especially clearly in the building programs of German universities. These were mainly conceived

56. *Christoph and Brigitte Parade: Secondary school, Menden, 1967–68.*

57. *Hans Joachim Pysall and Eike Rollenhagen: Westhagen Educational Center, Wolfsburg, 1967–68.*

at a time when the traditional authoritarian system was under the sharp attack of critics whose aim was the formulation of a new partnership between teacher and student. Thus it is hardly surprising that many of the new projects provoked violent opposition.

Such was the case with one of the largest undertakings of this sort, the University of the Ruhr in Bochum. While the overall planning is in the hands of the architects Helmut Hentrich and Hubert Petschnigg, the office of Eller, Moser, and Walter is responsible for individual buildings (*Fig. 61*). Criticism has been leveled at the schematic arrangement of the massive blocks intended to house the various institutes and at the lack of assimilable spatial scales.

The Bochum scheme contrasts sharply with the planning of the Free University in Berlin, one of the most interesting projects to be sponsored by the German universities *(Figs. 59–60)*. The winners of the design competition, a group consisting of Georges Candilis, Alexis Josic, and Shadrach Woods, took as their premise a high level of adaptability. With the object of enabling the college to respond easily to whatever future demands might be made upon it, they devised an essentially horizontal infrastructure to which two- or three-story units can be added as required. The total effect is of a relatively homogeneous, tapestry-like structure which, though it includes numerous open spaces, has no aggressive dominant forms. All this might equally well be interpreted as a complete denial of the great educational institutions' traditional claims that their image expresses

58. *Harald Deilmann: J. F. Kennedy Educational Center, Duisburg, 1966–69.*

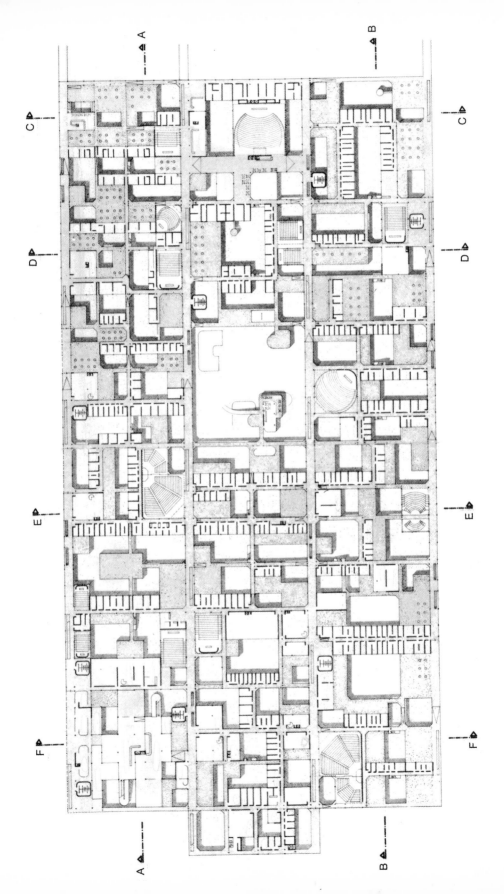

A
B
C
D
E
F
A
B
C
D
E
F

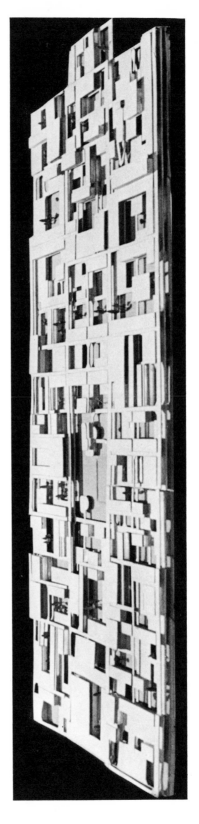

B B

ORGANIC CHEMISTRY

HISTORY

E E

GERMAN STUDIES

GERMAN STUDIES

PHILOSOPHY

F F

PSYCHOLOGY

GERMAN STUDIES

ENGLISH AND ROMANCE
LANGUAGES, BALCONY

DINING HALL

59. Georges Candilis, Alexis Josic, and Shadrach Woods with M. Schiedhelm: Free University, West Berlin, 1966–70, plan.
60. Free University, model.

the source of the nation's intellectual strength. When this campus is completed, the term "university atmosphere" may take on an entirely new significance.

In contrast to Bochum, the planning of Bremen University (*Fig. 62;* Fritz Eller, Erich Moser, Robert Walter, Nailis, Schmideknecht, Trebotic, and von Twickel, architects) is centered around a well-organized comblike structure based on a fixed grid into which buildings can be inserted as required. The campus itself is an area of relatively high density, while the housing areas are more loosely integrated.

Modular planning is also a feature of Marburg University (*Fig. 63*). Horizontal and vertical planning grids have been superimposed on the entire site. In spite, or possibly because, of this, the resulting structure is lively and dense. A particularly impressive aspect of Marburg is the carefully thought-out system of prefabricated parts,

61. *Helmut Hentrich, Hubert Petschnigg, Bochum office (Thoma and Thurn, job leaders): University of the Ruhr, Bochum, 1966–70.*

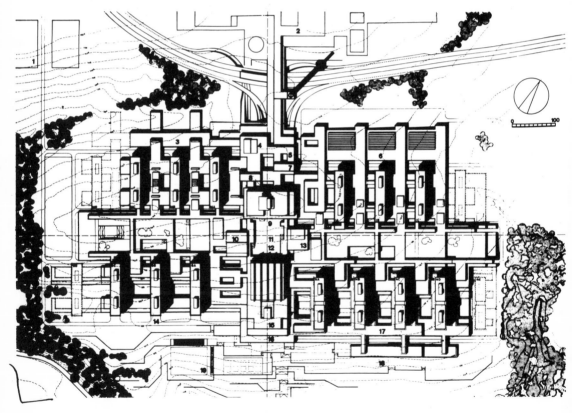

1. Clinic	7. University administration	13. East lecture room complex
2. City fringe	8. Library administration	14. Moral sciences
3. Theoretical medicine	9. Library	15. Dining hall, cafeteria
4. Music center	10. West lecture room complex	16. Tavern, games
5. Student housing	11. Forum	17. Natural sciences
6. Engineering sciences	12. Main auditorium	18. Botanical garden
		19. Sports ground

which, besides being economical, imposes architectural discipline and facilitates logical growth.

Apart from these large-scale projects, countless individual buildings have been erected as part of various college expansion and improvement programs. Friedrich Kraemer's still-unfinished complex for Brunswick Technical University, with its remarkable auditorium (*Fig. 64*), is typical of the architectural attitudes of the fifties, in its frankly economical means, simple structural system of concrete columns and supporting beams, and its large glass elements between the columns.

However, the trend toward a strongly expressive architecture capable of creating plastic values is traceable to 1960. The Law and Economics Building of the University of the Saarland in Saarbrücken (*Fig. 65*; Albert Dietz and Bernhard Grothe with Ralf Heinz Lamour, architects) is notable for its clearly conceived closed plan. Design accents are provided by the *brise-soleils*, which enliven the facade of the exposed concrete structure.

Engineering Structures and Industrial Buildings

Technical recovery in Germany was remarkably rapid, and high standards were reached only a few years after the end of the war.

Though German engineers have at one time or another employed every modern building technique, their mastery of prestressed concrete has been particularly impressive. The firm Dyckerhoff and

62. *Fritz Eller, Erich Moser, Robert Walter, with Nailis, Schmideknecht, Trebotic, and von Twickel: Bremen University, Bremen, 1967, model.*

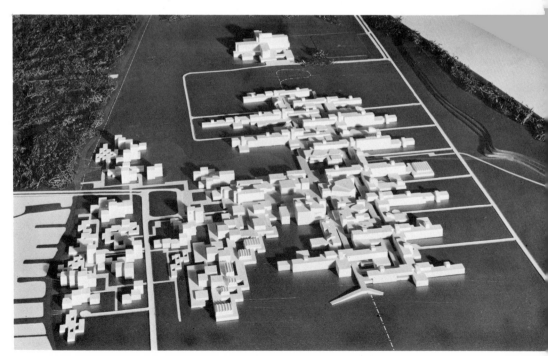

63. *University New Construction Committee with Kurt Schneider, Winfried Scholl, Helmut Spieker, Günther Nieduk, Bondzio, Herold:* Marburg University, Marburg, 1964–70.

64. *Friedrich W. Kraemer: Brunswick Technical University, 1961.*

Widmann pioneered in the development of this versatile new material, to which the engineers Franz Dischinger and Ulrich Finsterwalder have also devoted most of their working lives. Finsterwalder was the designer of the Elztal Bridge (*Fig. 66*), an example of mushroom slab construction.

At over 208 meters, the Rhine Bridge at Bendorf (Dyckerhoff and Widmann, in collaboration with Gerd Lohmer; *Fig. 67*) is the longest concrete girder span in the world. A bridge notable for its striking appearance as well as its technical virtuosity is the Severin Bridge across the Rhine at Cologne (*Fig. 68*; Gerd Lomer, architect). The steel cables that support the roadway are strung from a single mast.

In the area of industrial architecture, Walter Henn has been acclaimed for a series of buildings that are not only functional but also important achievements in design as well. In his Mechanical Engineering Institute for Brunswick Technical University (*Fig. 69*), technical requirements have been accentuated, deliberately shaped, and raised to the level of a refined technical aesthetic that recalls the work of Mies van der Rohe or the early Eero Saarinen. At the same time, there is an obvious interest in imaginative structures that, in addition to permitting material economics, have a strong visual appeal. The Deckel Engineering Plant in Munich by Walter Henn has a roof that spans sixty meters and provides excellent lighting.

65. *Albert Dietz, Bernhard Grothe with Ralf Heinz Lamour: Law and Economic Science Department, University of the Saarland, Saarbrücken, 1963–65.*

66. Dyckerhoff and Widmann (Ulrich Finsterwalder, chief engineer): Elztal Bridge, Elz Valley, 1965.

67. Dyckerhoff and Widmann (Gerd Lohmer, architect): Rhine Bridge at Bendorf, 1962–65.

The complex curves of the concrete roof of the Lohr Iron Foundry (*Fig. 70*), by Curt Siegel and Rudolf Wonneberg, reflect the level of sophistication achieved by modern thin-shell design. By creating a natural draft, the roof shape helps ventilate the foundry floor and at the same time floods it with light. The structural, economic, and functional requirements have thus been given convincing architectural expression in a unique creative synthesis of rational and formal elements.

The spirit of aestheticizing perfectionism is particularly apparent in the industrial projects of Hans Maurer. His workshop building for the Siemenswerk Research Center in Erlangen (*Fig. 71*), though not without a certain quality, typifies the technical emphasis and rationalism of this trend, which has an increasing following in Germany.

68. *Gutehoffnungshütte, Sterkrade AG (Gerd Lohmer, architect): Severin Bridge across the Rhine, Cologne, 1958–60.*

69. *Walter Henn: Mechanical Engineering Institute, Brunswick Technical University, 1967.*
70. *Curt Siegel and Rudolf Wonneberg: Lohr Iron Foundry, 1960–61.*

71. *Hans Maurer: Workshop building, Siemenswerke Research Center, Erlangen, 1965.*
72. *Fritz Schupp: "Germania" Mine, Dortmund, 1954.*

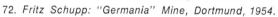

Where the form is determined by certain specific requirements, the architectural solutions are clear and simple—for example, in the mines of the Ruhr (*Fig. 72*; Fritz Schupp, architect). Schupp has employed harsh brickwork and a sharply articulated steel construction.

Munich is the site of one of Germany's biggest concrete structures, a parcel-post handling shed with a clear span of 147 meters (*Fig. 73*). Another noteworthy building is Ludwig Leo's sports stadium in Berlin-Charlottenburg. The precast concrete structure spans 50 meters.

The Wedel Power Station near Hamburg (*Fig. 74*), designed by Bernhard Hermkes, has an unconscious air of almost sacral solemnity which it owes to its lofty shed roofs and towering chimneys. A similar effect is produced by the sheer scale of the concrete shells that cover Hamburg's Central Market.

New transportation buildings to handle the increasing volume of air traffic have provided other architectural opportunities. The Cologne-Bonn area is to be served by an airport designed by Paul Schneider-Esleben (*Fig. 75*). The comprehensive passenger-handling facilities and star-shaped satellite buildings should ensure a level of efficiency unique in Europe. As in the United States, the style leans away from mannerism toward expressive monumentalism.

Otto Apel, Hansgeorg Beckert, and Gilbert Becker have made novel use of the familiar suspension principle in their design for an

73. *Dyckerhoff and Widmann: Parcel-post handling shed, Munich, 1966–68.*

aircraft hangar at Frankfurt am Main (*Fig. 76*). The roof members, which span fifty-five meters, are tied back to a central trestle.

The vigorous juxtaposition by architects Georg Heinrichs and Hans C. Müller of massive service towers and a two-dimensional, linear core structure in the Louis Leitz Factory, Stuttgart (*Fig. 79*), has parallels in the industrial architecture of England and the eastern United States.

The Foreign Contribution

Anyone observing the German architectural scene over the last ten years would have to admit that a very substantial contribution has been made by architects from abroad. The work of the Interbau group, Le Corbusier's Unité, and Mies van der Rohe's work are notable examples, as well as the Marl Town Hall by J. H. van den Broek and J. B. Bakema.

Alvar Aalto has built a church and cultural center (*Fig. 77*) in Wolfsburg (the Volkswagen city), the "Neue Vahr" high-rise apartments in Bremen (*Fig. 78*), and a church in Detmerode. Arne Jacobsen is planning an administrative building for the Hamburg Power Company; Philip Johnson has designed a compact museum for Bielefeld.

An important school building, the Ulm School of Design, is the work of a Swiss architect and artist, Max Bill. His clear uncompro-

74. Bernhard Hermkes: Wedel Power Station, near Hamburg, 1964.

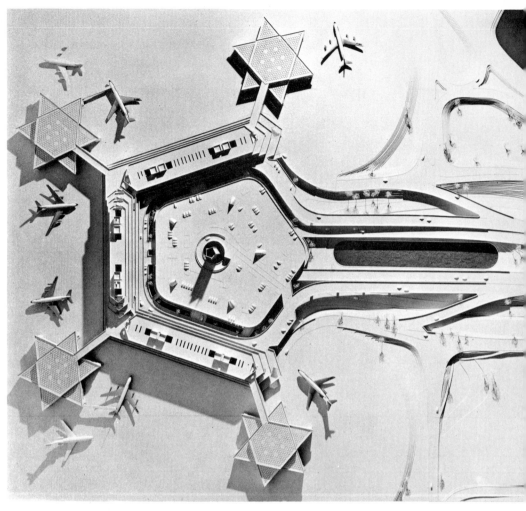

75. *Paul Schneider-Esleben: Cologne-Bonn Airport, 1966–70.*

76. *Otto Apel, Hansgeorg Beckert, and Gilbert Becker: Lufthansa hangar, Frankfurt am Main, 1965.*

mising conception here has something of the spirit of the prewar Bauhaus. The Congress Hall, Berlin, is based on a design by the American architect Hugh Stubbins. However, the structural principle was found impossible to follow consistently, and, structurally at least, the resulting form lacks conviction. The seemingly free shell requires additional supporting members, so that the dynamic sweep of the roof is actually faked.

Richard Neutra was commissioned to plan housing developments at Quickborn near Hamburg and at Walldorf near Frankfurt. The new city halls at Bremen (*Fig. 80*; with M. Säume) and at Ludwigshafen were designed by the Viennese Roland Rainer. In both instances the logic of the concrete structure becomes an expressive symbol of urban society.

Although these influences have their counterpart in the work of German architects abroad, it is questionable whether in this connection one can talk in terms of a "German architecture."

77. *Alvar Aalto: Wolfsburg Cultural Center, 1962.*
78. *Alvar Aalto: "Neue Vahr" apartments, near Bremen, 1962.*

79. *Hans C. Müller and Georg Heinrichs: Louis Leitz Factory, Stuttgart, 1966.*
80. *Roland Rainer (Vienna), M. Säume, and G. Norer: City Hall, Bremen, 1962–65.*

HOUSE, CITY, COMMUNITY

From House to City

JUST as college design is concerned with the material as well as the intellectual "universitas," at many other levels the boundary between the individual and the collective, the house and the city, is becoming increasingly blurred. As the integrating concept of terrace, step, and stair is acquiring new importance, an ancient architectural motif is being dusted off and put back on display.

In the A.R.A.G. Building in Düsseldorf (*Fig. 81*), Paul Schneider-Esleben has applied the stair motif to the offices of an insurance company. Here the utility of the terraces is of less consequence than the striking design. Paul Baumgarten has arrived at a similar solution for an apartment house in Detmerode near Wolfsburg (see "City Planning," p. 75), and Hans Joachim Pysall and Eike Rollenhagen employ stepped construction in their design for the offices of a publishing house now being built in Berlin.

This idea, consistently pursued, leads to the concept of the "Wohnberg," an artificial hill on which houses are built. Compared with some of the bolder proposals, actual accomplishments are, to be sure, rather modest—for example, the apartments in Marl (*Fig. 82*) designed by Roland Frey, Hans Schmidt, and Hermann Schröder (Peter Faller and Hermann Schröder, execution).

One of Erich Schneider-Wessling's projects (*Fig. 83*) is conceived along these lines; the hotel in Bad Godesberg is a cautious step in the same direction, a slice of a dwelling-hill, as it were.

The crater dwelling is like an inverted pyramid. Ulrich S. von Altenstadt and Gerhard Boeddinghaus have proposed this new "superform" for the development of Lohbrügge-Nord in Hamburg (*Fig. 84*). Routine city planning must, of course, content itself with less daring models.

City Planning

However tragic the destruction wrought by the Second World War, it did afford a unique opportunity for the complete rebuilding of cities. Unfortunately, working out an effective city plan is a lengthy process, and much of the work of reconstruction could not be postponed. For this reason, the majority of German cities were simply rebuilt along the same lines as before, with various obvious traffic improvements but with little in the way of true city planning innovations.

In some cases of development on smaller self-contained sites,

81. *Paul Schneider-Esleben: A.R.A.G. Insurance Company Building, Düsseldorf, 1967.*

82. *Roland Frey, Hans Schmidt, and Hermann Schröder (Peter Faller and Hermann Schröder, executive architects): Apartments, Marl, 1967.*

83. *Erich Schneider-Wessling: "Wohnberg" project, montage.*

84. *Ulrich S. von Altenstadt and Gerhard Boeddinghaus: Lohbrügge-Nord development, Hamburg, 1961, proposal.*

where a unifying master plan could be imposed, it frequently proved possible to achieve excellent space-mass relationships of notable aesthetic quality. As examples of such smaller accomplishments, one might mention the housing for the staff of Wildbad Hospital (*Fig. 85*), designed by Hans Kammerer and Walter Belz, or the charming solution of G. and M. Hänska for a small agricultural settlement (*Fig. 86*) on the edge of Gropiusstadt in Berlin. Here it is not just the Mediterranean associations evoked by the white cubes, but rather the deft handling of space and the relationship between the building masses and the open areas that make this an important model for the smaller type of organic development.

The problems of urban redevelopment on a large scale can be illustrated with reference to three examples taken from Berlin.

One of the first big city planning efforts of the postwar period was the reconstruction of the Hansa quarter in Berlin on the occasion of the Berlin International Building Exhibition, or Interbau, of 1957 (*Fig. 87*). Contributions were made not only by German architects but also by many top-ranking international designers as well. These included J. H. van den Broek and J. B. Bakema, Walter Gropius, Alvar Aalto (*Fig. 88*), Oskar Niemeyer, Arne Jacobsen, and, above all, though outside the Hansa quarter proper, Le Corbusier with a Unité (*Fig. 89*) which, regrettably, was badly executed. Despite the quality of the individual buildings, there is little to pull them together; they stand in lonely isolation between broad expanses of green, and the initial enthusiasm, probably inspired as much as anything by the scale of the project and the prestige of the architects, has long since turned to sharp criticism.

Seven years later a new project was launched in the Britz-Buckow-Rudow district of Berlin. This development for a total of fifty thousand people bears—no doubt unfairly—the name of Gropiusstadt. Walter Gropius' plan, the very basis of which was disputed, was variously modified until there finally arose a seemingly random collection of individual buildings with only flashes of architectural quality. In spite of the occasional urban intimacy of scale and here and there a particularly pleasing solution, it is impossible to discern any real progress. The planning sticks to the old principle of independent blocks, standing in isolation or at best in small groups. There is almost no visible evidence of overall spatial planning.

Construction also continues on the Märkisches Viertel, a housing development in Berlin (*Fig. 90*). Here at last it is possible to make out a meaningful forthright overall plan developed around an impressive center with its own marketplace. The entire site is bound together by landmarks and identifiable structures grouped around individual subcenters. The many bright urban design ideas incorporated in the Märkisches Viertel, which also includes a number of architecturally distinguished groups of houses, were conceived by Werner Düttmann, Hans C. Müller, and Georg Heinrichs.

85. *Hans Kammerer and Walter Belz: Housing for hospital staff, Wildbad, 1967.*

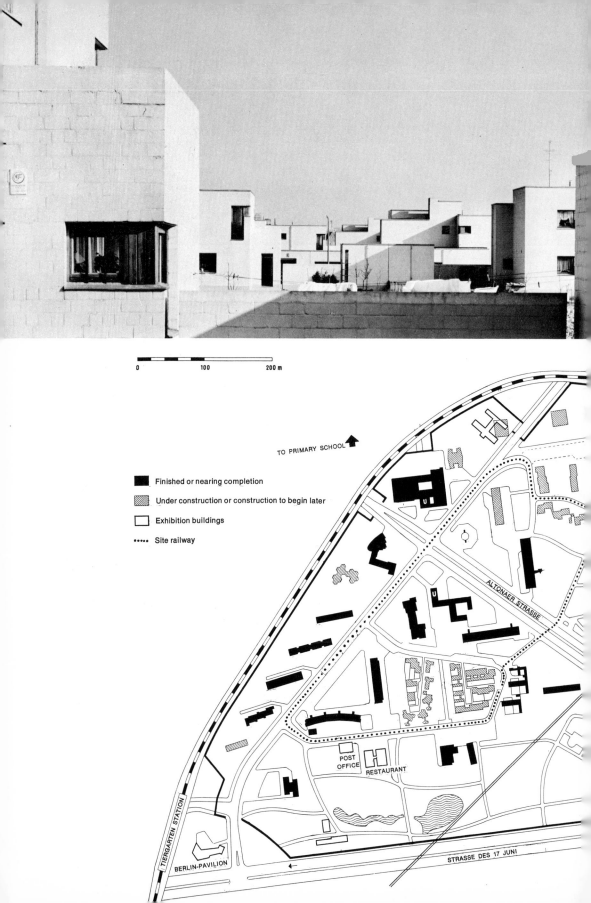

0   100   200 m

TO PRIMARY SCHOOL ⬆

■   Finished or nearing completion

▨   Under construction or construction to begin later

☐   Exhibition buildings

•••••   Site railway

ALTONAER STRASSE

TIERGARTEN STATION

POST OFFICE

RESTAURANT

BERLIN-PAVILION

STRASSE DES 17 JUNI

86. *G. and M. Hänska: Agricultural settlement, West Berlin, 1965–66.*
87. *Interbau Exposition, Hansa quarter, West Berlin, 1957, site plan.*

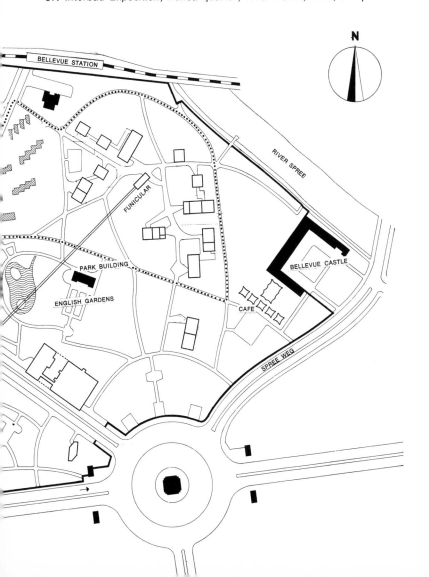

88. *Alvar Aalto: Apartment house, Interbau Exposition, West Berlin, 1956–57.*
89. *Le Corbusier: Unité d'habitation in Berlin, West Berlin, 1956–57, detail.*

The final plan for Nordweststadt near Frankfurt am Main (*Figs. 91–92*; Walter Schwagenscheidt and Tassilo Sittmann, architects) was the outcome of a whole range of sociological, humanitarian, and romantic considerations. The aim was a "human" solution somewhere between the extremes of the garden city and high-density planning. But today it is hard to distinguish any difference from an ordinary urban fringe development or satellite town characterized by a lack of human scale or intimacy, a lack of contact with city culture, social and functional disintegration, and poorly coordinated open spaces.

Near Wolfsburg another new town is being built: Detmerode. The residential planning is chiefly in the hands of architects' cooperatives. Efforts are being made to achieve a more vigorous plastic

90. *Werner Düttmann, Hans C. Müller, and Georg Heinrichs: Märkisches Viertel, West Berlin, 1964–71, site plan.*

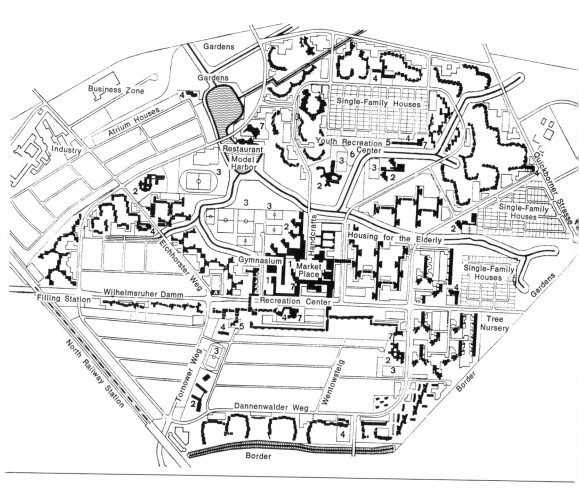

1. Center
2. Schools
3. Sports grounds
4. Kindergarten
5. Maintenance
6. Day nursery
7. Churches, parish centers

91. *Walter Schwagenscheidt and Tassilo Sittmann: Nordweststadt, Frankfurt am Main, 1961–70, secondary centers.*

92. *Nordweststadt, site plan.*

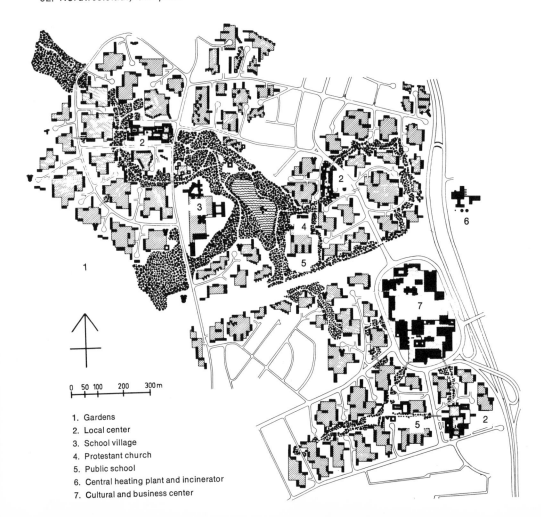

1. Gardens
2. Local center
3. School village
4. Protestant church
5. Public school
6. Central heating plant and incinerator
7. Cultural and business center

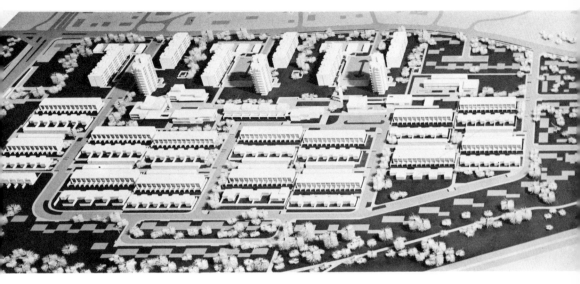

93. *Wolfgang Hirsch, Rudolf Hoinkis, Martin Lanz, Paul Schütz, and Dieter Stahl: Baumgarten residential area, Karlsruhe, 1965–70, model.*

94. *Baumgarten residential area, detail of apartment building.*

expression, and special care is being taken with such key follow-up structures as the schools, churches, and shopping centers.

In contrast to most satellite towns and suburban developments, the Baumgarten residential district of Karlsruhe (*Figs. 93–94*; Hirsch, Hoinkis, Lanz, and Schütz, architects) has a strict, rectangular town plan, which is effectively relaxed by the liveliness and excellent design of the buildings and open spaces.

So-called "tapestry" planning, in which low, flat houses and spaces are woven together in a continuous fabric, is an attempt to escape from the amorphous jumble of the outer suburbs and dormitory towns. Reinhard Gieselmann offers an excellent example in Karlsruhe West, which is particularly notable for its use of open space. A multifamily dwelling by the same architect (*Fig. 95*) would make a good prototype for higher-density urban construction. Finally, the Bethany Children's Village near Bensberg (*Fig. 96*; Gottfried Böhm, architect) is also a poetically conceived urban grouping. The concentric development, which forms a series of handsome plazas, has the central chapel as its focus.

The architect Merete Mattern has shown that a highly individual poetry of space and volume has its place even in city planning (*Fig. 97*). However, her design involves more than a mere play of forms; rather, it is intended to act as a stimulant for new social possibilities. Urban space is envisaged not as a rigid framework for existing society, but as offering a new range of possibilities: the buildings are not permanently "frozen"; on the contrary, they can be modified and manipulated and are perpetually involved in a process of metamorphosis.

Community and Society

Unlike in East Germany, where social problems are formulated by the Party ideologists (see "East Germany"), in the West the new society and its architectural manifestations are the subject of sharp public debate. The issues include the social relevance of architecture and the dangers of potential political manipulation of design and architecture.

In urban design, the predestined battleground for clashing sociological forces, the decisions reached so far have been both disappointing and incomplete. The new systems are still in the embryonic state.

Naturally, the problems of smaller, sociologically more cohesive groups are more easily solved. There are several notable examples of student housing. Peter Lehrecke groups sixteen-unit student apartments around a well-organized and handsomely proportioned interior court, one function of which is to act as an outside play area for the children of married students. A convincing example of the student community is the youth hostel in Berlin (*Fig. 98*) by Hans C. Müller and Georg Heinrichs.

95. *Reinhard Gieselmann: Multifamily dwelling, Karlsruhe-Durlach, 1965–66.*
96. *Gottfried Böhm: Bethany Children's Village, Bensberg, 1966–68.*

Homes for the aged also afford good opportunities for reflecting social content in architecture. In Karlsruhe (*Fig. 95*), Reinhard Gieselmann has tried to formulate a key problem in architectural terms: how to preserve the privacy of the individual and respect his right to choose and organize his own environment, while at the same time relate him to a lively but unobtrusive community.

The needs of contemporary society appear to be even more clearly formulated in the numerous community halls and social centers that are springing up as centers of urban life not only in the new towns but also in the old cities. A convincing example is Günther Bock's design for a community center in Sindlingen (*Fig. 33*).

The planning of these buildings reflects the varied needs of the community, particularly those relating to its recreational, cultural, and political activities. Besides a large and a small auditorium, Peter Voigtländer's community center for Brunswick includes a restaurant and a café, information and press rooms, exhibition areas and lecture halls, club rooms and conference rooms.

One of the most outstanding contemporary manifestations of an urban society on German soil, Marl Town Hall (*Figs. 99–100*), is the work of the Dutch firm of Van den Broek and Bakema. This building, which, for all its functionalism, offers an abundance of architectural experiences, is genuinely representative of a self-assured society, capable of erecting proud symbols of its power and importance. The council building is approached by a broad

97. *Merete Mattern and assistants: Urban design study for Ratingen, 1965.*

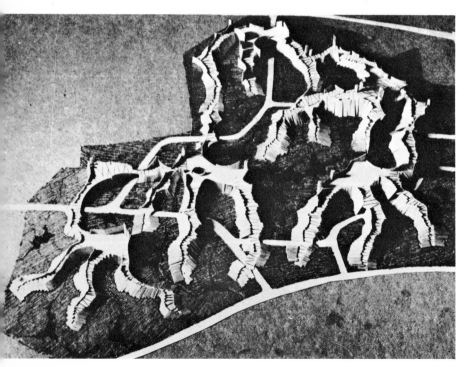

flight of stairs. Its impressive folded roof shelters the council chambers and meeting rooms. The administrative offices are in two towers (two more will eventually be added) designed on the suspension principle. The main buildings are linked by a well-articulated chain of subordinate masses and open spaces.

To some extent, sports buildings also visually express the ideals of the new society, since sports fans make up one of the few groups with members drawn from every social class. The Mainz Swimming Bath (*Fig. 101*) with its long-span folded plate roof, by Otto Apel, Hansgeorg Beckert, and Gilbert Becker, may be regarded as a solution determined by the interesting choice of structural system.

All the facilities of a comprehensive town center are to be found in Nordweststadt near Frankfurt am Main (*Figs. 102–103*; Otto Apel, Hansgeorg Beckert, and Gilbert Becker, architects). Here there has been an obvious effort to sprinkle the new developments with points of urban concentration in an attempt to achieve a complex interweaving of individual functions. The result is an architecturally highly differentiated, lively scheme that could help drive out the dismal planning typical of so many urban fringe developments and satellite towns. The many different levels also provide a variety of spatial experiences in the vertical plane. Thus, cultural and commercial, educational and social requirements are combined in a new synthesis.

98. *Hans C. Müller and George Heinrichs: Youth hostel, Tiergarten, West Berlin, first section 1962, second section 1966.*

99. *G. H. van den Broek and Jacob Bakema: Stadtkrone (town hall), Marl, 1967, general view.*
100. *Stadtkrone.*

The question remains: What importance should be accorded the individual detached house? However severely it may be criticized by the younger generation of architects, it is still the dream of an increasingly affluent society, a dream which appears to take two main forms: a rustic cottage or a sentimental luxury villa. Few buildings succeed in rising much above this level. One of the best to do so is a house near Cologne (*Fig. 104*), designed by Joachim Schürmann, which depends for its effect on an array of stepped terraces and white-painted concrete cubes. The future appears to be brighter for row and cluster housing. The group of atrium houses developed by Harald Deilmann for Bad Duisburg (*Fig. 105*) is characterized by the alternation of concrete and brick.

The social aspects of modern architecture are being most severely criticized by the younger generation, and there can be no doubt that from these critical attitudes there will ultimately emerge a completely new conception of the sociological role of architecture.

101. *Otto Apel, Hansgeorg Beckert, and Gilbert Becker: Swimming bath, Mainz, 1960–62.*

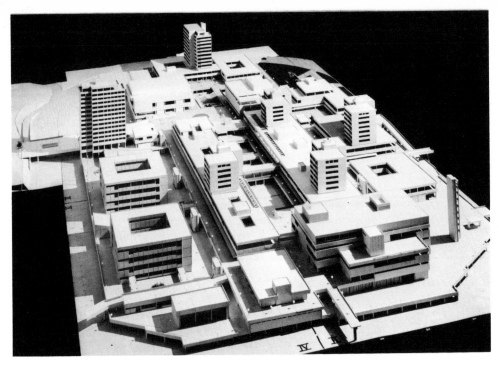

102. *Otto Apel, Hansgeorg Beckert, and Gilbert Becker: Town center, Nordweststadt, Frankfurt am Main, 1966–69, model.*

103. *Town center, Nordweststadt, detail.*

104. *Joachim Schürmann: K. residence, near Cologne, 1967.*
105. *Harald Deilmann: Atrium houses, Bad Duisburg, 1962.*

TECHNOLOGY

Residential Construction and Prefabrication

A SPECIAL interest of the younger architects is the development of prefabrication. This interest includes not only the economies that prefabrication is supposed to provide, but also a specific design philosophy.

The idea of prefabrication was rather slow to take hold in West Germany, and as a result the number of prefabricated buildings is much smaller than in other European countries. Moreover, no master system has yet been developed for residential construction, for example. In fact, the variety of systems available, which would be impossible to consider individually, has impeded the rational application of the prefabrication principle.

One of the few genuine experiments that has succeeded in getting off the drawing board is one devised by Wolfgang Döring. The prefabricated units that form this house (*Fig. 106*) were erected in five days. The result proves that this method of construction can also lead to pleasing architectural effects, derived in this instance from the striking emphasis on the process of structural assembly.

The Hochdahl Housing Estate near Düsseldorf (*Fig. 107*; Fritz Eller, Erich Moser, and Robert Walter, architects), though largely prefabricated, seeks to avoid the mournful look of many such developments by varying the window types and vigorously articulating the buildings in solid rows, while still keeping within a limited budget.

New Techniques

In the area of new building techniques, as with urban design, most of the interest centers on projects still on the drawing board or in the early experimental stage. However, in the next few years many of these studies, calculations, and small-scale tests will doubtless bear fruit.

One of the most important personalities on the German scene is Frei Otto, engineer, architect, researcher, and theoretician. Although he can scarcely be said to design "buildings" in the conventional sense and although his work has had little impact on the routine operations of the German construction industry, he deserves the credit for an entirely new approach to the problem of providing "shelter." Like R. Buckminster Fuller, his concern is with enclosing large spaces with the minimum amount of material. Frei Otto specializes in tensile-stress construction and derived systems. His extensive experiments with tentlike structures culminated in his

106. *Wolfgang Döring: M. K. residence, Bad Honnef / Rhein, 1967.*

107. *Fritz Eller, Erich Moser, and Robert Walter: Residential development, Hochdahl-Kolksheide, near Düsseldorf, 1966–68.*

imposing design for the German pavilion at Expo 67 in Montreal (*Figs. 108–109*), a dynamic landscape of wide-spanning tent forms that not only have an interesting silhouette but also create marvelous interior spaces. Frei Otto believes that the techniques employed in his tent structures can be extended to city planning solutions, even to the enclosing of whole regions.

The way in which Otto works is clearly revealed in his study for a roof over a swimming bath. The original suspension model (*Fig. 110*), stressed purely in tension, is used to derive a shell form whose static behavior is then investigated on an experimental structure (*Fig. 111*). The complete roof is represented by a model (*Fig. 112*) showing the arrangement of the individual shell elements.

Apart from shells and tents, another of Frei Otto's interests, one which he shares with many younger architects, is inflated structures (*Figs. 113–114*), whose potential uses include exhibition halls, armories, and shelters for expeditions.

Frei Otto's big tent at Expo 67 is the prototype for facilities now being planned for the 1972 Olympic Games in Munich. Günther Behnisch & Partners (Fritz Auer, Winfried Büxel, Erhard Tränker, Karlheinz Weber) propose to stretch huge tentlike roofs (*Fig. 115*) over the various arenas, which will be constructed largely by excavation. Viewed as a whole, the structure is intended to form not a colossal mass, but an articulated unit that blends with the existing landscape. The superform of the tents loosens and binds, opens and closes.

Gernot Minke, a former collaborator of Frei Otto's, has developed the idea of "Wohnberg" in a theoretical example incorporating the suspension principle (*Fig. 116*).

108. *Frei Otto: German pavilion, Montreal Expo 67, 1967, exterior view.*

109. *German Pavilion (Rolf Gutbrod interior design), interior view.*

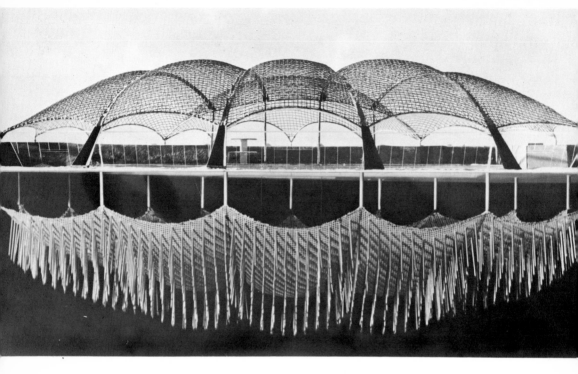

110. *Frei Otto: Study for a swimming bath roof, 1967, structural system (above), static test (below), models.*

111. *Swimming bath roof, experimental structure.*

112. *Swimming bath roof, complete model.*
113. *Frei Otto: Pneumatic structures, model.*
114. *Pneumatic structures, model.*

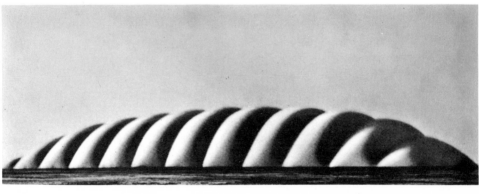

The space frame is another important new building technique that has caught the imagination of German architects and engineers. Working along the same lines as Konrad Wachsmann (now an American citizen), the engineer Max Mengeringhausen developed and successfully marketed the Mero system, a simple steel-framework system with great flexibility which is now used extensively, especially for temporary and mobile structures.

Eckhard Schulze-Fielitz used this system to build St. James in Düsseldorf (*Figs. 117–119*), probably one of the most important and influential buildings in Germany. In spite (or possibly because) of the strict logic of the structure, the interior has, one must admit, a "sacral" dignity and finally exposes the triviality of the argument concerning the relative importance of the technical and artistic elements in modern architecture.

Like Yona Friedmann in France, however, Schulze-Fielitz has chiefly been preoccupied with the design of space frames with important applications for city planning. These systems are intended to span enormous distances and form cages within which various

115. *Günther Behnisch & Partners (Fritz Auer, Winfried Büxel, Erhard Tränker, Karlheinz Weber): Facilities for the 1972 Olympic Games, Munich, 1968–71.*

functional and living units can be organized in different three-dimensional arrangements.

Germany is moving in the direction of a universal concept of architecture, but first satisfactory answers must be found to a number of pertinent questions. What possibilities of free disposability and variability can a structure incorporate? What are the technical means available? What are the orders of magnitude involved? What is the importance of growth processes and how can they be made possible? To what extent can living and technical functions be combined? The latter theme is imaginatively handled in Schulze-Fielitz's scheme for a bridge over the English Channel (*Figs. 120–122*; with Yona Friedmann). Utopian? The technical means have long been available, and the idea of interweaving homes and transportation systems is now being repeatedly brought up.

Schulze-Fielitz demonstrates the variability inherent in the space lattice in his proposals for the University of the Ruhr in Bochum (*Fig. 123*). The unity and multiplicity of the university are simultaneously expressed.

The ultimate in mobility, namely, motion of the entire spatial system, is realized in Schulze-Fielitz's project for a floating exhibition (*Fig. 124*). Here again it is a question of a germinal idea: there is no reason why the system should not be extended to projects on an urban scale, to veritable floating cities.

This same strange blend of structural logic and exuberant imagination, as displayed by Frei Otto and Schulze-Fielitz, also appears in the work of another interesting personality: Günter Günschel. His project for a domed structure composed of hyperbolic paraboloids (*Fig. 125*), which dates from 1957, was conceived as a great sphere set in the countryside and sheathed in transparent

116. *Gernot Minke: "Wohnberg" designed as a suspension structure, 1965–68.*

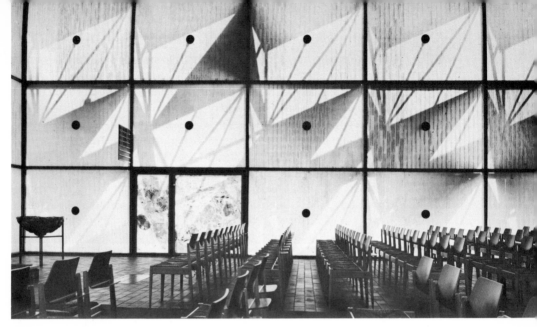

117. *Eckhard Schulze-Fielitz: St. James, Düsseldorf-Eller, 1960, interior.*
118. *St. James, during construction.*
119. *St. James, interior structure.*

120. *Eckhard Schulze-Fielitz and Yona Friedmann: Project for a bridge city over the English Channel.*
121. *Project for a bridge city over the English Channel.*
122. *Project for a bridge city over the English Channel.*

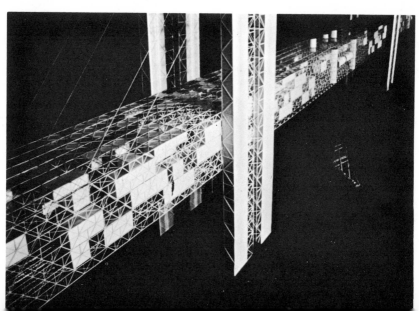

123. *Eckhard Schulze-Fielitz: University of the Ruhr, Bochum, 1962, competition entry.*

124. *Eckhard Schulze-Fielitz: "Arche," floating exhibition pavilion, study for Montreal Expo 67, 1964.*

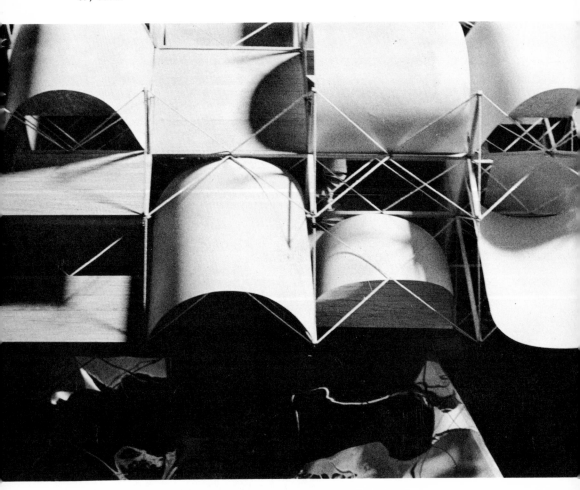

plastic. This form, a further development of studies with tetrahedra, recalls Buckminster Fuller's huge geodesic domes.

The new roof of the Church of the Epiphany in Berlin (*Fig. 126*), by Konrad Sage and Karl Hebecker, is a modest variation on the space frame principle in which the weight-saving properties of structural aluminum are also exploited.

Mobility and Flexibility

The younger generation of German architects has two main sources of inspiration: the sociological implications of architecture and the new technology. In particular, it is the problem of functional and structural variability that underlies many of the more imaginative proposals, which of course for the time being exist only on paper. One means of achieving extreme flexibility is illustrated, for example, by Johannes Peter Hölzinger's design (with Herman Goepfert) for a lakeside restaurant to form part of a garden show (*Fig. 127*). Fluorescent tubes are inserted into a supporting steel frame at different levels.

Wolfgang Rathke's "monostructure" (*Fig. 128*), which in this instance functions as a fair pavilion, would be built of numerous small, possibly variable, interlocking elements. Variability is carried to the extreme in the permanent building site (*Fig. 129*) of a university project developed by Rathke in collaboration with Lyubo-Mir Szabo and H. Behrendt: a permanent gantry crane provides for rapid reconstruction and continual adaptation to changing circumstances.

New Materials

New materials can be just as influential as new structural techniques. Paradoxically, though Germany has a highly sophisticated plastics industry, experiments with plastics building elements have so far been limited. This has been attributed to the architects' lack

125. *Günter Günschel: Project for a domed structure composed of hyperbolic paraboloids, 1957, photomontage.*

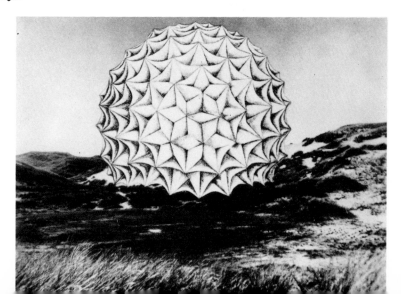

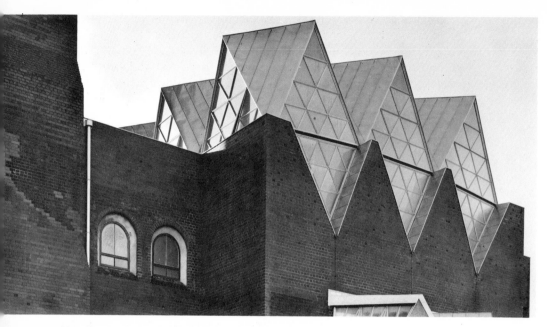

126. *Konrad Sage and Karl Hebecker: Church of the Epiphany, West Berlin, new roof, 1960.*

127. *Johannes Peter Hölzinger and Hermann Goepfert: Lakeside restaurant, garden show, Karlsruhe, 1966–67.*

128. *Wolfgang Rathke: Study for a "monostructure" for Montreal Expo 67, 1964.*

129. *Wolfgang Rathke with L.-M. Szabo and H. Behrendt: Plan for Bremen University, 1967.*

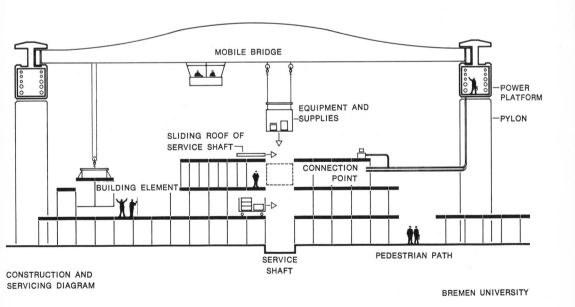

MOBILE BRIDGE

POWER PLATFORM

PYLON

EQUIPMENT AND SUPPLIES

SLIDING ROOF OF SERVICE SHAFT

CONNECTION POINT

BUILDING ELEMENT

SERVICE SHAFT

PEDESTRIAN PATH

CONSTRUCTION AND SERVICING DIAGRAM

BREMEN UNIVERSITY

130. *Ralf Schüler and Ursulina Witte: Experimental house of plastics construction, 1967.*
131. *Wolfgang Döring: Building constructed from polyester cells, stacked and stressed, 1966.*

of interest. But the designers who do make use of plastics do so not only for technical reasons but also out of fascination with the material.

The experimental house designed by Ralf Schüler and Ursulina Witte (*Fig. 130*) explores the entire range of combinational possibilities with special emphasis on vertical applications. A number of other ideas are also in the experimental stage. For apartment towers, Wolfgang Döring is testing a stack of polyester "cells" tensioned with steel cables (*Fig. 131*); in another of Döring's systems, these units are inserted in a supporting frame.

Dieter Schmid's handling of plastics in his house at Biberach (*Fig. 132*) has received much favorable comment. The design respects the true nature of the material, which is also used for most of the fixtures, and from this derives its undeniably excellent, unconventional, formal qualities. In a series of highly promising technical and design studies (*Figs. 133–135*), Schmid has indicated how the use of plastics as building materials for houses, schools, and community centers is likely to develop. Plastic shells are also used in larger elements, and the designer's imagination has been fired by the many possibilities offered by the new material.

132. *Dieter Schmid: Plastics house, Biberach, 1967.*

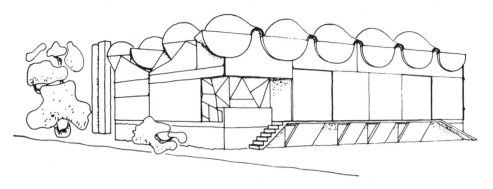

133. *Dieter Schmid: Studies for plastics houses, 1966–68.*

134. *Studies for plastics houses.*

135. *Studies for plastics houses.*

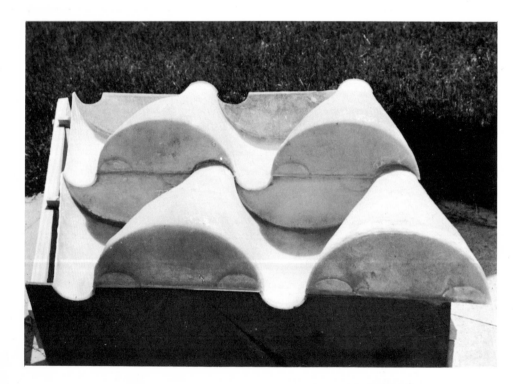

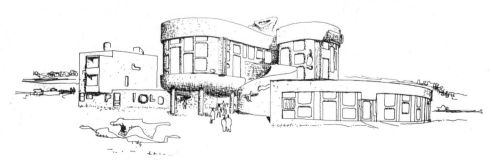

EAST GERMANY

Residential Construction and Urban Design

TO DO justice to the situation in East Germany, one must use a set of standards different from that for West Germany. Application of the sociological and aesthetic criteria that have been developed specifically in the West would doubtless lead to unfavorable conclusions.

In East Germany (Deutsche Demokratische Republik), a socialist state, the political and economic basis of building and city planning is totally different. Public ownership of industry, the emphasis on a planned economy, and one-party rule mean that all planning measures are subject to rigorous centralized official control.

However, when one inquires how such a socialist society finds tangible expression in its architecture, one immediately experiences considerable difficulty in discerning any fundamental differences from the architecture of the West. Certainly East German planning lacks the commercial exuberance typical of a capitalist economy, but the elements of business, consumption, and even advertising are present nonetheless. In particular, there is a surprising affinity with the latest Western ideas toward sociological requirements. Community centers, open spaces, government complexes, and recreational facilities are needs felt equally in East and West.

Although a planned economy creates a different framework within which the construction industry must operate, the political coloring of the system is surprisingly faint; it is scarcely possible to speak any more of a specifically "socialist city planning" in any Communist country, particularly East Germany. Except for the episode of Moscow-oriented Stalinist architecture, more bourgeois than revolutionary in its attributes, today's proposed solutions display a definite affinity with West German planning. The efforts of socialist theoreticians to set East German architecture apart from that in the West are unconvincing.

In the city centers themselves, one sometimes encounters a structure more severely hierarchic and centralized than is customary in the West. One criterion is suggested by the prevalence of broad open spaces—"squares" occasionally too vast even to be recognized as such—no doubt envisaged as arenas for great political parades and demonstrations. However, the concept of a "socialist living complex" has little validity as a social criterion.

The first concern of city planning was with minor projects such as reconstruction of row-houses. The official style of Moscow-oriented, paradoxically bourgeois architecture set the tone for the construction of the first part of the Stalinallee (now Karl Marx Allee) in Berlin, a city soon to be brought to an extreme pass by its fateful division into two parts, East and West, by the Wall. The extension of Karl Marx Allee (*Figs. 136–137*) reveals genuine urban ambitions. This section of the boulevard is characterized by cinemas and restaurants, hotels and stores. The famous street Unter den Linden was also spruced up in the course of activities connected with the restoration of historic buildings.

In the late fifties the Altmarkt in Dresden, the center of Magdeburg, and the Lange Strasse in Rostock were the objects of limited urban renewal programs.

In the late fifties the Altmarkt in Dresden, the center of Magdebasic policies: on the one hand, the decision to standardize certain types of residential buildings, which has generally led to severely geometric, rigid housing patterns; and, on the other, the decision to emphasize community facilities in the city centers. The plans for these centers include such facilities as shops, restaurants, bars, and recreation and amusement areas, all familiar to the West. Although the trend toward a conscious development of open spaces is crystallized in the later designs, the urge to create huge squares suitable for mass political gatherings now appears somewhat more restrained.

A typical example is the design for the central square of Karl Marx Stadt (*Fig. 138*), the work of a team from the Weimar Architectural School, consisting of Peter Andrä, Klaus Griebel, Walter Krätze, Erhard Schmidt, and Wolfgang Schmutzer. Cultural and entertainment buildings form the core of the program, but the square itself is dominated by the big Communist Party building; office construction of a Western type appears in the tower for the National Enterprises. When the project was redesigned by a team of architects headed by Rudolf Weiser (*Fig. 139*), an obvious attempt was made to compensate for the general boxiness by a more lively grouping of the central buildings. The architectural content of the buildings themselves has also been reinterpreted.

The plan for the new town of Schwedt (*Fig. 140*) makes similar provisions for the town center, and particular importance is attached to the sports areas, so that the site as a whole is typically spacious and loosely articulated, indeed somewhat disconnected.

The almost unmanageable detail and scope of many city planning schemes have been kept effectively under control in the new project for the center of Hoyerswerda (*Fig. 141*; Dresden Technical University, H. Trauzettel).

Although the urban design projects of the sixties are based on carefully organized competitions, the results may still appear highly schematic or monotonous. The proposals for the chemical workers' city of Halle-West, intended to house 35,000 people (*Fig. 142*), show very plainly that the ideas of the city planners have not yet progressed beyond a schematic, essentially rectangular arrangement of elongated apartment blocks. This basic approach, derived from a

136. *Josef Kaiser: Karl Marx Allee extension, Hotel Berolina and Cinema International, East Berlin, 1960–62.*

137. *Josef Kaiser: Housing on Karl Marx Allee, East Berlin, 1963.*

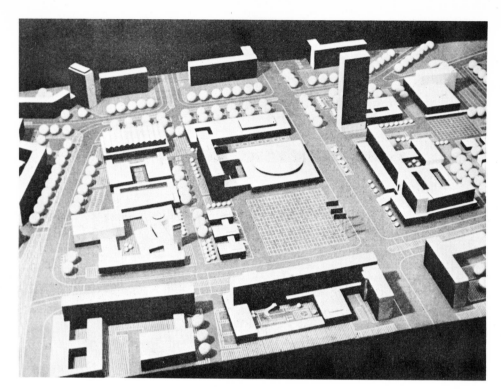

138. *Peter Andrä, Klaus Griebel, Walter Krätze, Erhard Schmidt, and Wolfgang Schmutzer (collective of Weimar Architectural School): Prize-winning entry in design competition for the central square of Karl Marx Stadt (formerly Chemnitz),*

139. *Rudolf Weiser collective: Central square, Karl Marx Stadt (formerly Chemnitz), East Germany, 1966, revised plan.*

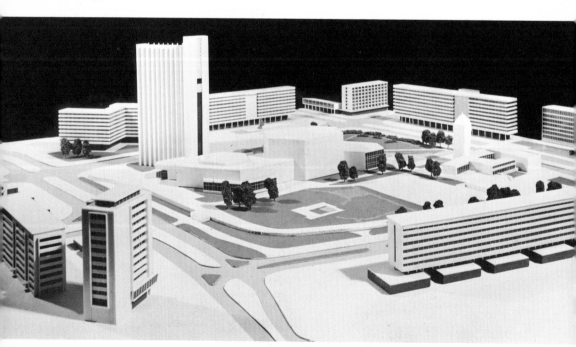

RESIDENTIAL
CONSTRUCTION

1. Kindergarten	15. Inn
2. Day nursery	16. Swimming pool
3. 20-class school	17. Hospital with ambulance and pharmacy
4. Special classes, lunchroom	18. Handcraft area
5. Gymnasium, locker rooms	19. Railroad station
6. Cultural center with hotels	20. Parking areas
7. Movies, espresso, fashions	21. Parking garage
8. Administration	22. Schoolyard
9. Post office, insurance, savings bank	23. Exercise area
10. Department store	24. Gymnastics
11. Car showroom	25. Baseball and basketball
12. Specialty shops	26. School garden
13. Food stores	27. Volleyball
14. Hotel	28. Playing field

140. *Design Office for Regional, Town, and Village Planning: Development plan for the town of Schwedt, East Germany, 1960.*

141. *Dresden Technical University (Professor H. Trauzettel): Housing complex and community center, Hoyerswerda, East Germany, 1967.*

142. *Institute for City Planning and Architecture, German Building Academy: Development plan for Halle-West, East Germany, 1964.*

143. *Heinz Graffunder and Wolfgang Radtke (residential and commercial construction). redevelopment of center of East Berlin with TV tower, 1965–70, model.*

trend of rationalization and standardization, is also to be found in the large-scale development planned by the V.E.B. (Volkseigene Betriebe) Industrieprojektierung for Rostock-Lütten/Klein.

From the outset, any attempt at an unorthodox treatment of space and form (for example, in the Heinrich Heine quarter of Berlin, which seeks a more lively disposition of housing blocks) encounters strong opposition. Western methods of achieving new spatial relationships and a new sense of identification are accepted only after much hesitation, and moreover, the bourgeois provincialism of the Stalin era has persisted as a standard of design into the sixties.

The growing Western trend toward higher urban densities is scarcely perceptible in the projects that have been completed so far in the East. There, for the most part, tight clustering is avoided even in the central cities. The latest designs, however, appear to mark a sharp reversal from monotonous row and block construction, and Western experiments with new urban and spatial forms are being debated.

The centers of gravity of inner-city renewal are Berlin, Dresden, Leipzig, and Frankfurt an der Oder. The plan for the center of East Berlin (*Fig. 143*) envisages a loving restoration and revitalization of existing historic buildings, again a reflection of corresponding attitudes in the West. The reconstruction of Berlin's Alexanderplatz (*Fig. 144*), with its shopping center, hotel and restaurant, and office and administrative buildings, has genuine urban potential. The TV tower, which soars to a height of 360 meters, will become a new landmark in East Berlin. Some of the buildings are already finished and, for all the efforts to achieve a modern international look, betray a concern for artistically handcrafted accents that comes dangerously close to Western kitsch. Nor are the attempts at integrating architecture and modern art altogether successful. For example, in the Haus des Lehrers (Teachers' Assembly and Education Center) on Alexanderplatz (*Fig. 145*; Hermann Henselmann, architect), a remarkably ambitious building, the image of a socialist society has not been satisfactorily projected.

Social Architecture

Surprisingly, the so-called "social" buildings, with the possible exception of certain community centers and educational institutions, rarely succeed in expressing a recognizable social image. The characteristics of a classless, a Communist, and a socialist society—a united working class—find no meaningful expression in the architecture. Certainly, innovation is only hesitantly accepted.

The projection of images of power and authority, usually associated exclusively with the West German affluent society, does have its counterpart in the East, not only in the economic and political sphere—as illustrated by the Foreign Ministry Building in East Berlin (*Fig. 146*)—but also in the cultural sphere. The new Opera House in Leipzig (*Fig. 147*) is a striking example of how the denunciation of Stalinist architecture in no way implies the rejection of bourgeois representational attitudes. The architectural details are remarkable for their often clumsy traditionalism.

Even the notion of collectivism, however, is expressed in only a small number of buildings of technically superior quality. A possible example is the Zentralgaststätte (Central Inn) in Berlin, whose vast dining rooms can seat over three thousand people.

Hotels are also "social" buildings in the broader sense. In an attempt to please the tourist, the latest hotels strive for an international standard and a certain lavishness, without displaying any specifically socialist characteristics. The Hotel Deutschland in Leipzig (*Fig. 148*) and the Hotel Berolina in Berlin are typical examples.

Cubic-plastic design trends are usually dismissed as formalism or accepted only with reluctance. The first shy experimentation with

144. *Joachim Näther (city planning), Roland Korn (high-rise hotel): Redesign of Alexanderplatz, East Berlin, 1964–70, model.*

145. *Hermann Henselmann and others: Teachers' Assembly and Education Center, East Berlin, 1964–66.*

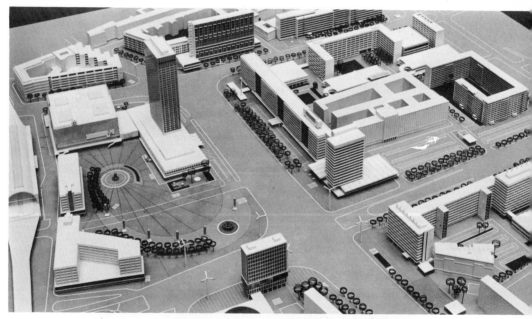

these ideas may be observed in a refectory building at Dresden Technical University (W. Rössler, architect).

Prefabrication

Like all the states of Eastern Europe, the German Democratic Republic has a keen interest in the economic advantages of prefabrication. Surface decoration, often inadequate, is employed in an effort to alleviate the monotony of long lines of identical apartment blocks and row houses. Much of this construction is of the wall panel type, common throughout Eastern Europe and also in France.

Unit construction systems are also being closely studied. In this case, the principle is to use a small number of basic manufactured units that can be fitted together to obtain a variety of architectural effects. The building block system, in which room-size modular units

146. *Josef Kaiser: Foreign Ministry of the Deutsche Demokratische Republik, East Berlin, 1966.*
147. *Kunz Nierade: Opera House, Leipzig, East Germany, 1960.*

are put together in various combinations, is also believed to have considerable potential.

The trend toward standardization is naturally stronger than it is in the West, being less subject to individualistic or ideological constraints. Attention is concentrated less on aesthetics and more on the problems of rationalization. The necessary experience is being accumulated in extensive pilot projects; nonetheless, for the last ten years the often inferior quality of much urban and architectural design has been the source of considerable dissatisfaction.

Industrial Buildings

The problem of reconciling functionalism and aesthetics is of little moment to East German industrial architects and engineers whose main concern is with structural rationale. Nonetheless, they have produced a number of interesting solutions, notably a hangar at the East Berlin airport (Brigarde Richter, architect; V.E.B. Industrie-projektierung Dessau), whose arched concrete shell roof members span cantilevered prestressed concrete box girders.

148. *Helmut Ullmann, Wolfgang Scheibe: Hotel Deutschland, Leipzig, East Germany, 1965.*

149. *Herbert Müller, Wolfgang Fraustadt, Armin Menzel, and others: Warehouse, Sangerhausen, East Germany, 1964.*

150. *Bernhard Altenkirch (V.E.B. Industrieprojektierung Berlin 1): Power station, Lübbenau, East Germany, 1964.*

Another notable roof structure is that covering a Berlin bus garage (G. Franke and H. Kissing, architects; K. Reitzig and U. Wurzbacher, structural engineers; V.E.B. Industrieprojektierung Berlin 1). This is a suspended roof with a span of more than fifty meters. Hyperbolic paraboloid shell construction has occasionally been used —for example, in a warehouse at Sangerhausen (*Fig. 149*; Herbert Müller, Wolfgang Fraustadt, Armin Menzel, architects).

Industrial buildings sometimes provide examples of "accidental architecture," strictly utilitarian, aesthetically neutral buildings which the human mind may nonetheless choose to find "beautiful." One such structure is the heating plant of the big Lübbenau Power Station (*Fig. 150*; Bernhard Altenkirch, architect).

FUTURE PROSPECTS

WHAT are the prospects for German architecture?

It is scarcely possible to predict coming developments in architecture with absolute accuracy. One can merely speculate on the directions in which the younger generation is most likely to move. The creative younger architects have two main concerns: city planning and the immediate human environment, which they interpret broadly to include the urban image of street and square, mobile capsules and flexible elements, furniture and appliances, public art, and the visual manifestations of commercial and economic interests such as advertising. In all these areas the influence of sociological factors is strong.

Thus, it is reasonable to expect an extensive revision and redefinition of the sociopolitical frame of reference, which may have far-reaching effects on architecture and city planning.

Stefan Wewerka is a forceful representative of the new generation. His interesting plan for the residential area of Ruhwald (*Fig. 151*) attempts to revive, in a contemporary modification, the unfashionable city-street row-house theme, while his decentralization of services in netlike structures suggests new possibilities in urban design.

Intellectually, the younger architects are torn between two apparent extremes: at one pole lie individuality, fantasy, poetry, even sentimentality, and at the other science, systems analysis and computerization, research and technology, industrialization, and theory, whose ultimate aim is the objectivization and quantification of architecture.

Something of what may be in store can be glimpsed in the work of Johannes Uhl. By means of analytical drawings and the compositional criteria that he derives from them, this intriguing young architect is trying to arrive at a new method of design. He has certainly been successful in demonstrating the extraordinary complexity of the design process, which he represents schematically in diagrams of unusual graphic interest. Uhl's comparison of his compositions with a "part song" is intended to underscore the fact that creative thinking must proceed on several levels at the same time. His work is marked by a graceful but wayward poetic fantasy, often cryptic, enigmatic, and abstract (*Fig. 153*). His specific proposals for the Berlin Museums (Fig. 152), for example, are in fact characterized by a bold complexity and a resourceful use of forms, the outcome of his profoundly analytical approach.

Like Uhl, virtually every younger architect is preoccupied with

151. *Stefan Wewerka: Proposal for residential area, Ruhwald, 1964, model.*
152. *Johannes Uhl: Berlin Museums competition, 1966, model.*

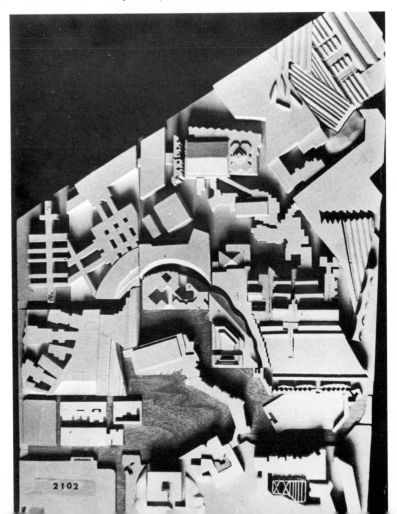

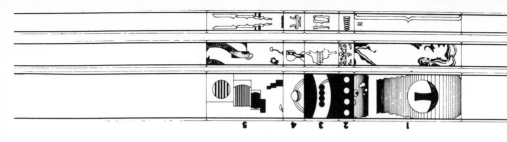

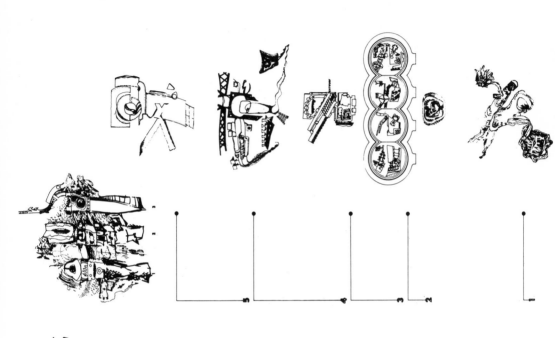

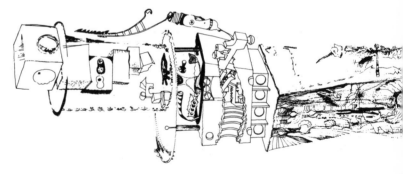

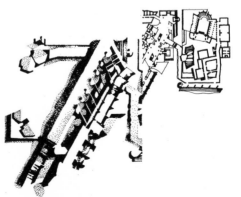

153. Johannes Uhl: Analytical drawing-compositional study-"part song" for collaboration (proposal for German-French high school), 1966.

city planning. Klaus J. Thiele and Ludwig Leo are representative of this group. Among the younger architects with a number of completed projects already to their credit, an important place must be assigned to the team of Gerd Neumann, Dietmar Grötzebach, and Günter Plessow. For all their obvious sympathy with Brutalism in its more subdued forms, their individual designs, despite certain idiosyncrasies, are quite undogmatic. Their motel in Berlin-Grunewald (*Fig. 154*) is proof that even structurally rich differentiation can be reconciled with a disciplined conception of the whole. The effect is reminiscent of some recent British work which retains an appealing gravity despite the broken volumes. The same austerity also permits industrial motifs to be smoothly incorporated in the design for a school (*Fig. 155*) or it can be dynamically allied with diagonal elements as in the community center in Berlin's Märkisches Viertel (*Fig. 156*).

One of the few projects to exploit the new spatial experiences derived from audio-visual techniques and from structures that move is the theater proposed by Wolfgang Döring (*Fig. 157*). Images are projected on variable plastic surfaces to the accompaniment of a sound track; the audience platform can be rotated and pivoted about its supporting pillar.

This suggests just one of the many possible extensions of the idea of architecture. Its function will no longer be merely that of providing shelter and giving visual expression to political, cultural, and economic power but will involve the exploration of new regions of experience, new states of consciousness. Eventually, a strong psychological element will take its place beside the sociological factors on which interest is currently focused.

New and expanded methods of communication and the potential of images and illusions projected by electronic means will combine with the concepts of flexibility and mobility in fascinating and original trends. For the time being, however, most of this must remain on a theoretical basis. But if the activities and ideas that now preoccupy the younger German architects, and particularly the students, bear fruit, there is likely to be a radical change in the architectural scene within a relatively short while.

154. *Gerd Neumann, Dietmar Grötzebach, and Günter Plessow: Motel, Berlin-Grunewald, 1966–68.*

155. *Gerd Neumann, Dietmar Grötzebach, and Günter Plessow: Protestant school, Charlottenburg, West Berlin, 1967, proposal.*

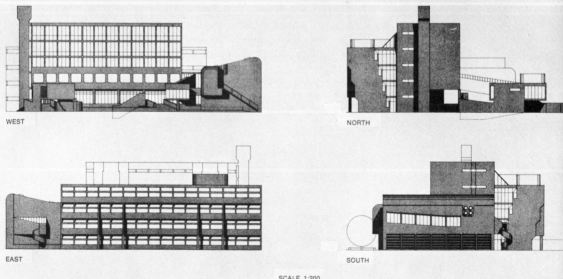

WEST

NORTH

EAST

SOUTH

SCALE 1:200

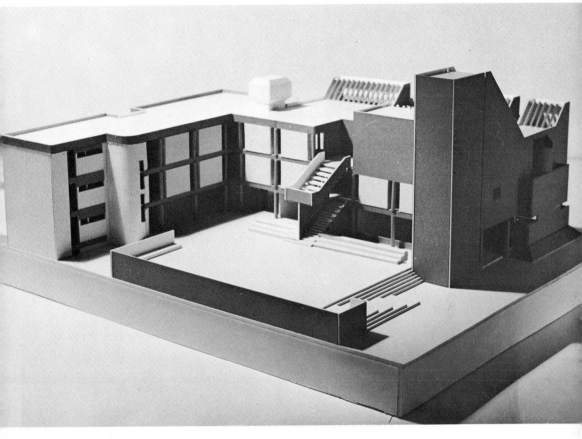

156. *Gerd Neumann, Dietmar Grötzebach, and Günter Plessow: Community center, Märkisches Viertel, West Berlin, 1967.*

157. *Wolfgang Döring: Theater project, 1968.*

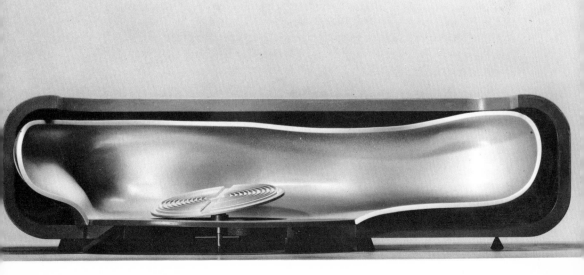

BIBLIOGRAPHY

Books

Banham, Reyner. *Guide to Modern Architecture*. London, 1962; New York: Van Nostrand, 1963.

Conrads, Ulrich, and Marschall, Werner. *Neue Deutsche Architektur*. Stuttgart, 1962. (*Contemporary Architecture in Germany*. New York: Frederick A. Praeger, 1962.)

Donat, John (ed.). *World Architecture One*. London: Studio Vista, 1964.

————. *World Architecture Two*. London: Studio Vista, 1965.

Fengler, Max. *Heime*. Stuttgart, 1963. (*Students' Dormitories and Homes for the Aged*. New York: Universe Books, 1964.)

Hassenpflug, Peters. *Scheibe, Punkt und Hügel*. Munich, 1966.

Hatje, Gerd (ed.). *Lexikon der modernen Architektur*. Munich, 1966.

————. *Neue deutsche Architektur*. Stuttgart, 1956. (*New German Architecture*. London: Architectural Press, 1956.)

Henn, Walter. *Industriebau. Internationale Beispiele*. Munich, 1962.

————. *Sozialbauten der Industrie*. Munich, 1966.

Jacobus, John. *Die Architektur unserer Zeit*. Teufen, 1966.

Joedicke, Jürgen. *Bürobauten*. Stuttgart, 1959. (*Office Buildings*. New York: Frederick A. Praeger, 1962.)

————. *Geschichte der modernen Architektur*. Teufen, 1958. (*A History of Modern Architecture*. New York: Frederick A. Praeger, 1959.)

Kellen, D. *Internationale Architekturdokumentation*. The Hague, 1965.

Kidder-Smith, G. E. *The New Architecture of Europe*. New York: World Publishing Company, 1961.

————. *The New Churches of Europe*. New York: Holt, Rinehart and Winston, 1964.

Kultermann, Udo. *Baukunst der Gegenwart*. Tübingen, 1958.

————. *Neues Bauen in der Welt*. Tübingen, 1965. (*New Architecture in the World*. New York: Universe Books, 1965.)

Mittag, Martin. *Thyssenhaus*. Essen, 1962.

Pichard, Joseph. *Modern Churches*. Paris, 1960.

Rave, R., and Knöfel, H. J. *Bauen seit 1900—Ein Führer durch Berlin*. Berlin, 1963.

Ruf, Sep. *German Church Architecture of the 20th Century*. Munich, 1964.

Schulz, Eberhard. *Die Prediger mit dem Reissbrett*. Stuttgart, 1964.

Schwarz, Rudolf. *Kirchenbau*. Heidelberg, 1960.

Periodicals

Bauen und Wohnen, Munich.

Bauwelt, Berlin.

DB (Deutsche Bauzeitung–Die Bauzeitung merged with *Baukunst und Werk-form)*, Stuttgart.

DBZ (Deutsche Bauzeitschrift), Gütersloh.

Werk, Winterthur.

L'architettura, Rome.

Aujourd'hui, Boulogne. (Suspended publication; see especially no. 57/58.)

L'architecture d'aujourd'hui, Boulogne.

INDEX

SOURCES OF ILLUSTRATIONS

O. Apel and G. Becker: 101
Archiv für Kirchenbau und
Kunst, Vienna: 17
J. B. Bakema and J. H. van
den Broeck: 99
Inge Bartholomé, Aachen: 96
© Ulfert Beckert, Offenbach
am Main: 102, 103
© Beton-Verlag, Peter Fischer,
Düsseldorf-Oberkassel:
24
G. Beygang, Karl Marx Stadt:
139
J. Billings, J. Peters, N. Ruff:
53
© Brecht-Einzig Ltd., Richard
Einzig, London: 85
Gudrun Bublitz: 93
G. Candilis: 59
D & W archives: Eiselt
(Munich), 73; Ohlsen
(Bremen), 80; Stiebel
(Koblenz), 66, 67
Deutsche Architektur, Berlin:
138, 140, 142, 145, 147,
149, 150
Deutsche Bauzeitung (Foto G.
Mangold, Bonn): 84
W. Döring: 106, 131, 157
W. Düttmann: 15, 90
Walter Ehmann, Cologne-
Klettenberg: 38
© Rudolph Eimke, Düsseldorf:
39
Jupp Falke, Frankfurt am
Main: 33
G. Feuerstein, Vienna: 6, 8, 9,
11, 14, 28, 32, 34, 50, 61,
72, 74, 78, 88, 89
G. Feuerstein, files, Vienna: 13,
16, 40, 87, 137, 143, 144,
151
H. Fiebich, Berlin-
Johannisburg: 136

Paul Förster, Offenbach am
Main, 65
Foto-Bruggemann, Leipzig: 148
Foto-Deyhle, Rottenburg: 79
Foto-Hatt, Stuttgart: 10
Foto-Kessler, Berlin-
Wilmersdorf: 4, 55
© Reinhard Friedrich, Berlin:
49, 86, 98
Ewald Glesmann, Munich: 115
© Inge Goertz-Bauer,
Düsseldorf: 2, 58, 62, 75,
107
Max Göllner, Frankfurt am
Main: 76
Marianne Gotz, Stuttgart-
Hohenheim: 26
Gutehoffnungshütte: 68
Robert Häusser, Mannheim-
Käfertal: 22, 23, 27, 42
Heidersberger, Wolfsburg: 3,
69, 70
Hochtief AG, Essen: 100
J. P. Hölzinger: 36
© Nina von Jaanson, Berlin: 60
Klaus Kinold, Karlsruhe: 25,
54, 94
Hans König, Bad Nauheim: 127
F. W. Kraemer: 64
© Christoph-Albrecht Kühn zu
Reineck, Hamburg: 82
Dieter Lechner, Munich: 7
Wolf Lücking, Berlin: 5, 52
M. Mattern: 97
H. Maurer: 71
© Thilo Mechau, Karlsruhe-
West: 35, 95
Klaus Meier-Ude, Frankfurt am
Main: 91
G. Minke: 116
L. Mosso, The Museum of
Finnish Architecture,
Helsinki: 77
Rainer Müller, Berlin: 146
G. Neumann, D. Grotzebach,

G. Plessow: 154, 155, 156
F. Otto: 110, 111, 112, 113, 114
C. and B. Parade: 56
© Artur Pfau, Mannheim-
Feudenheim: 18
Photo-Meyer, Vienna: 108, 109
© Georg Prager, Frankfurt am
Main: 29
H. J. Pysall: 57
W. Rathke, Wuppertal-
Elberfeld: 128, 129
© Dieter Rensing, Münsing:
20, 21
Inge von der Ropp, Cologne:
19, 31
K. Sage and K. Hebecker: 126
H. Scharoun: 45, 46, 47, 48, 51
D. Schmid: 133, 134, 135
P. Schneider-Esleben: 81
E. Schneider-Wessling: 83
R. Schüler and U. Witte: 44,
130
E. Schulze-Fielitz: 117, 118,
119, 120, 121, 122, 123,
124
J. Schürmann: 43
W. Schwagenscheidt and
T. Sittmann: 92
Wolfgang Siol, Neu-Ulm: 132
Stadtbildstelle, Leverkusen: 41
© Helmut Stahl, Cologne: 30,
104
Friedhelm Thomas, Campione-
Lugano: 105
H. Trauzettel: 141
J. Uhl: 152, 153
O. M. Ungers: 37
Universitäts-Neubaumt: 63
Verlag Hatje, Stuttgart
(Conrads-Sperlich,
*Phantastische
Architektur*): 125
Rosemarie Wallrapp,
Oberhochstadt/Taunus: 12
Arno Wrubel, Düsseldorf: 1